LOOKING FOR A
New Pastor

LOOKING FOR A
New Pastor

---

10 QUESTIONS EVERY CHURCH SHOULD ASK

FRANK S. PAGE, PH.D.

B&H
PUBLISHING GROUP
NASHVILLE, TENNESSEE

Published by B&H Publishing Group
Nashville, Tennessee

Dewey Decimal Classification: 253
Subject Heading: PASTOR SEARCH COMMITTEE \
CLERGY

1 2 3 4 5 6 7 • 21 20 19 18 17

This book is dedicated to those wonderful churches where I have served, and the churches in the future that I hope I will be able to assist.

Acknowledgments

For a book such as this, which is highly pragmatic and based on years of experience in the local church, I must acknowledge the churches where I have been privileged to pastor. I served as student pastor in several churches in Texas, followed by pastorates at:

- Lafayette Baptist Church, Fayetteville, NC
- Gambrell Street Baptist Church, Fort Worth, TX
- Warren Baptist Church, Augusta, GA
- First Baptist Church, Taylors, SC

I am deeply indebted to those churches for many lessons learned, and have continued wonderful relationships with the persons in those churches to this day.

I also am grateful for the persons in the churches where I have been privileged to be an interim pastor. The men and women in these churches have taught me greatly and allowed me to gain much experience, some of which is reflected in this book. Those churches are:

- First Baptist Church, Jackson, MS
- First Baptist Church of North Augusta, SC
- First Baptist Church, Simpsonville, SC
- First Baptist Church, Brandon, FL
- Prince Avenue Baptist Church, Athens, GA

I also must acknowledge the wonderful assistance of Sharon Robinson, who is my primary personal Executive Assistant, and Becky Chandler, who is Senior Executive Assistant to the Executive Committee. These two ladies are a great encouragement to me and assist with many different areas and projects in my work and life. I am deeply grateful for their assistance, particularly Sharon, as she has helped with this manuscript from beginning to finish.

Contents

Introduction

Pastor Search for Dummies

 In recent years, millions of books on a variety of subjects have sold under the title _____ *for Dummies*. Though these titles may be offensive for some, they come as a relief to others. These books may deal with academic subjects such as mathematics or with issues in the spiritual realm such as Bible knowledge. I almost titled this book *Pastor Searches for Dummies*! I knew this title might offend some, but as I shared the title

> I almost titled this book *Pastor Searches for Dummies*!

with many, it seemed appropriate! Many, if not most, individuals who are involved in pastor searches are woefully unprepared and almost always inexperienced as they face one of the most important tasks in the life of a church.

Another subtitle could have been *What I Wish I Had Known*! This particular book is about helping the thousands of churches who find themselves every year without a pastor, senior pastor, or lead pastor, and do not know what to do, where to go, or how to start the process. There have been a few resources written, though not many, thus revealing that the need is indeed great.

There is no way to be completely certain about the number of churches in the United States, but estimates are pulled from surveys of various kinds. Most experts would say there are about 315,000 Protestant or non-Catholic churches and about twenty-five thousand Catholic or orthodox churches. Non-Christian religious congregations are estimated at more than ten thousand.[1]

In the Southern Baptist Convention context in which I serve, there are currently a few more than forty-six thousand churches. The sizes of these churches vary greatly—some average more than twenty-five thousand weekly attendees, while most average well under one hundred. In fact, to the surprise of many, the vast majority of churches, including Southern Baptist churches, are small. A recent survey of the Southern Baptist Convention's Annual Church Profile (ACP) shows that only 184 Southern Baptist churches average more than two thousand on a weekly basis. Most of the Kingdom work in the world is done by everyday, Jesus-loving, small churches!

According to Ed Stetzer, formerly of the LifeWay Christian Resources Research Division, roughly 10 percent of churches hire a new senior pastor yearly. If that is true across the nation, then one can easily understand the huge need for a book such as this one. This means that in the United States every year, on the low end of the spectrum, 31,500 churches are looking for a pastor. In the Southern Baptist Convention alone, that means more than forty-one hundred churches are looking for a pastor at any given point in time. The need is huge for assistance to churches that are looking for a pastor.

William Vanderbloemen, in his book *Search*, says there are generally three causes for the loss of the senior

pastor: emergency, retirement, or an unforeseen departure. Each of these affects the church and community in
different ways.[2] He is correct in those broad designations.

Why is there such a need? Why are so many pastors leaving a certain church or even the pastorate?
Why is there so much movement within this vocation?
No one knows for certain why pastors move. There is
often given a blanket "call of God" statement to cover
movement at any point in time. While I am not argu-
ing that a call of God is never the motivation for these
moves, I do know that it can become an easy cop-out
phrase and is often a cover-up for other issues. Indeed,
in a relatively recent study by LifeWay Research, a
"change in calling" was given as the reason why 40
percent of senior pastors left the pastorate.[3]

In that same article other reasons were given
for individuals' leaving the pastorate. This article
was referring to those who did not move to another
church but literally left altogether. Some of the reasons
described were as follows:

- No sabbatical provided
- No help with counseling cases
- No clear picture of what's expected from the
  church

- Conflict within the church
- Burnout
- Personal finances
- Family issues
- Church has unrealistic expectations
- Isolation in the ministry

Obviously the reasons for the massive amount of turnover and transition are many and varied. Indeed, there are numerous resources written on this subject. It should cause every church and minister to pause to consider what is happening within their church regarding pastor/church relationships. It should give all of us a wake-up call to reevaluate what is happening within our own fellowships and how we relate as ministers and laypersons. The bottom line is, many people are leaving the ministry. I was told when I was in seminary that in the next twenty to thirty years, two out of three people in my seminary class would no longer be in ministry. Whether that number is true or exaggerated, I know of many who have left over the years. As a result, the number of vacancies in churches is staggering.

Across the evangelical world these vacancies are going to increase in the days ahead. Many, if not most, in the current pastoral pool are approaching retirement. In many states this number is a large majority. It is encouraging on the one hand to know that there are record numbers of seminarians preparing for ministry in the Southern Baptist theological seminaries. On the other hand, this impending retirement of a significant number of pastors is going to leave many churches looking for a minister, and the churches may not be able to find many with experience or capability to lead them in the days ahead. Thus, the issue could become seriously problematic.

I have pondered this issue from a personal perspective. Many of my ministry friends over the years have left because of burnout and others because of moral or financial failure. However, the specific cause for most that I have seen is simply an inability to handle conflict and to persevere through the more difficult times of ministry. This seems to be an ongoing issue which needs to be addressed in our local fellowship.

I served as a full-time pastor for more than thirty-four years. I have now served in denominational work for more than eight, all the while serving as an interim pastor at various churches. I can assure you that over the years I have seen hundreds of examples of pastor searches gone right as well as those gone wrong.

There are multiple examples of churches who are like Jacob in the Old Testament. In Genesis 29, Jacob labored for seven years so he could marry Rachel. The morning after the wedding, to his amazement he realized his work was in vain. He had married her sister Leah! Many churches think they have acquired a Rachel, only to realize too late that they have hired a Leah. On the other hand, countless pastors have thought they were going to a Rachel church but after just a few weeks or months have realized they ended up with a Leah church!

I am not saying all poor hires involve a good church and a bad pastor or a good pastor and a bad church—though both certainly happen. What happens even more often, however, is that a good church hires a good pastor who just isn't a good fit. It is crucial, when searching for a pastor, that a church not only finds a good pastor but also the right pastor for that church.

Two examples come to mind of those times when searches have gone right and gone wrong. Some years ago, a large church in the South decided to follow their long-tenured pastor's advice and bring in a younger man to transition into the pastoral role. Things simply could not have gone more wrong.

Neither the tenured pastor nor his wife was willing to relinquish control, and the newer pastor simply could not handle the pressure of that situation. Since that time several pastors have come and gone, transitioning that church into a now successful, healthy church. Many years of devastating decline and defeat, however, came in the wake of that pastor's inability to let go of the reins.

Another example involves a church that experienced a similar transition with a pastor who was long tenured and very popular. That church, however, experienced a seamless transition as the long-tenured pastor was able to ease himself from leadership and allow the newer pastor to successfully take the reins, leading the church to an even greater day than it had previously experienced.

I have observed many examples of churches that have made good decisions and those who have made bad decisions. I have seen pastors who have done the same thing. This book will deal with these scenarios.

A sermon I enjoy preaching is titled "An Irrecoverable Moment." In this sermon I refer to a phrase Billy Graham used and reported in his autobiography, *Just as I Am*. Graham once met then

President-elect John F. Kennedy and had a discussion about spiritual issues. A few years later he met him again at the 1963 National Prayer Breakfast in Washington, D.C. President Kennedy asked Billy Graham to ride back to the White House and spend a few minutes with him. Unfortunately, Billy Graham felt that he had the flu and was physically weak and debilitated. "Mr. President," Graham told the president, "I've got a fever. . . . Not only am I weak, but I don't want to give you this thing. Couldn't we wait and talk some other time?"[4] Understandingly, the president gave him the opportunity to visit some other time. Billy Graham writes that there would be no other time as later that same year an assassin's bullet would cut short the life of that young president. Graham said in his book that he would forever regret that decision. He reflects that this moment for both President Kennedy and himself became "an irrecoverable moment."[5]

There are times when churches are called upon to make decisions that might well be described as irrecoverable moments. Churches have opportunities to make decisions that can shape their lives and future in a positive way or in a negative way. It is incumbent upon churches, therefore, to be serious, deliberate, and prayerful about their selection process. Many do not even know how to get started. Most do not know how to use resources available to assist them. Such is the need for this book. All of us need help, and wise men and women recognize that need and seek help where it is available.

This book assumes a congregational form of search where a team or committee is responsible for the nomination of the new pastor. This is by far the most common methodology by which a church finds its new pastor or minister, but it is not the exclusive methodology. Some churches do not have a congregational form but an elder structure, in which a small group of leaders govern the church body and also oversee the selection of the other elders, teaching pastors, lead pastors, or senior pastors. There are still other forms where the denomination is heavily involved in the appointment of new pastors. The principles found in this book may not be applicable where these other forms of church governance exist or where a church initiates a "transition plan" guided by the current pastor. This topic is covered in chapter 3 at some level; however, please recognize this book primarily deals with churches that have a congregational form of search.

What Does the Bible Say?

In the community of Southern Baptist Convention churches I serve, the issue of scriptural adherence and scriptural allegiance is one of paramount importance. For decades Baptists struggled in their corporate life with the issue of scriptural inerrancy. Those battles, though continuing at various levels, have been decided in most places. The vast majority of Southern Baptist leaders and congregants have a high view of scriptural integrity. Therefore, it is extremely important that this book begin with the question, "What does the Bible say?" Scripture is our guide for faith and practice and should certainly be our guide when it comes to hiring a new pastor.

God's Plan for Your Church

Let me begin by saying that God does have a plan for your church. I believe God has plans for individuals. Jeremiah 29:11 says, "'For I know the plans I have for you'—this is the LORD's declaration—'plans for your welfare, not for disaster, to give you a future and a hope.'" That often-quoted Scripture does indeed relay our Lord's desire for individuals and His promise that He has plans for us. I don't believe, however, that these plans stop with the individual; I believe they transcend to the corporate body of the church. If He has a plan for individuals, don't you think He has a plan for your local church?

> God does have a plan for your church.

Another meaningful passage is John 15:16 which says, "You did not choose Me, but I chose you. I appointed you that you should go out and produce fruit and that your fruit should remain, so that whatever you ask the Father in My name, He will give you." Isn't that a precious passage? Our Lord has chosen us for a purpose and saved us for a reason, and that is to bear fruit. Note that this fruit will last. Obviously, God has a plan, and His plan is that we would be fruitful in our ministries and lives.

The great passage that talks about the founding of the church is found in Matthew 16. In that passage Christ tells us of the founding of the church, and in verse 18 He clarifies, "On this rock I will build My church." Study that passage, and you will see that He is referring to Himself! In verse 19 Christ points out part of the plan for the church—that He will give us "the keys of the kingdom of heaven."

What are these keys of the kingdom? What do we do with them? I believe God's plan for the church is to make it the voice by which heaven is offered to men, women, boys, and girls. It gives the church an awesome responsibility in evangelism and ministry. Clearly, God has a plan for the church!

But God is not the only one with a plan for your church. Let me also hasten to say that Satan has a plan for your church as well! This frightens some people. I have stated on many occasions that every pastor search committee should be able to verbalize what Satan's plan is for their church. If we do not know the strategy of the enemy, how are we going to be able to combat him? John 10:10 speaks to the strategy of the evil one. The text says, "A thief comes only to steal and to kill and to destroy. I have come so that they may have life and have it in abundance."

As you are reminded in this passage, the evil one's strategy is "to steal and to kill and to destroy." How can Satan's plan be accomplished in your church as he works to steal the unity of your body? Call the wrong

> Satan has a plan for your church as well.

pastor and you will find out Satan can see this accomplished. How can Satan kill in your fellowship? If the wrong decisions are made, the evil one can use those decisions to kill the hopes for a future and to kill any forward momentum your church may have had. How can the thief destroy your church? Look around and see how many times dreams and encouragement have been destroyed by the evil one over the issue of the calling of a pastor and how that can discourage a church so quickly.

Making God's Plan Your Plan

I do not say these things in order to discourage but to bring you to an understanding of the reality that just as God has a plan, so does the evil one. We want to be people of the Book and follow the plan God has for us. We know we need to be serious in seeking to guard ourselves against the plans of the evil one, to recognize his footprints in our fellowship, and to diligently put on the full armor of God so that we might see God's victory in our churches!

Scripture not only gives us a good idea about God's plan for the church and a warning about Satan's plan for the church, but it also helps us know what we should look for in regards to a pastor and what we should expect from the pastor. In other words, the Bible helps us develop our own plan for our church that is consistent with God's plan.

Much has been written about Paul's words to Timothy in the book of 1 Timothy, specifically chapters 3 and 4. The advice he gives is extremely relevant for a twenty-first-century church. Listen carefully to what Paul says as he gives the job requirements for an overseer, which can also be described as a pastor, elder, or bishop. He "must be above reproach, the husband of one wife, self-controlled, sensible, respectable, hospitable, an able teacher, not addicted to wine, not a bully but gentle, not quarrelsome, not greedy—one who manages his own household competently, having his children under control with all dignity. . . . He must not be a new convert, or he might become conceited. . . . He must have a good reputation among outsiders" (1 Tim. 3:2–4, 6–7).

So we have our job requirements, but what about the job description? Many people ask about the job description of a pastor. Actually, Scripture provides it. It is found in Ephesians 4:11–13: "And He personally gave some to be apostles, some prophets, some evangelists, some pastors and teachers, for the training of the saints in the work of ministry, to build up the body of Christ, until we all reach unity in the faith and in the knowledge of God's Son growing into a mature man with a stature measured by Christ's fullness."

> Many people ask about the job description of a pastor.

Obviously, God has said that the role of the pastor and teacher is to prepare God's people for works of service that will "build up the body of Christ." Verse 13 describes a powerful goal that is the goal of every pastor. There are actually some churches where people think they hire a preacher to do all the witnessing, the ministering, the visiting, etc. That kind of mindset does not belong in the church and is completely contrary to that which is in the Word of God. All Christians should be involved in the work of ministry, both pastors and laypersons. The role of the pastor is not to do all of these works of service; it is to prepare God's people for these works of service! The works of service are universal in their assignment, but the pastor's role is unique in that he is the preparer, the equipper, or the trainer for service.

So, what does the Bible say? You should be looking for a pastor who has all the godly characteristics mentioned in 1 Timothy 3 and who is a great trainer, equipper, or teacher, according to Ephesians 4. If you are looking for someone who will do all the work, then you are not looking for a pastor in the biblical sense; you are looking for some kind of person who is not fulfilling the totality of God's command. Be careful that your church understands what God's Word says and be ready to follow and fulfill His Word so that you might be blessed by Him in every way. Spend time studying this during your interim phase.

We will discuss using a survey for the church later in this book. However, for now, let me share this. Before a congregation is surveyed about what they want or do not want in a pastor, it would be time well spent for the pastor search committee, elders, or church leaders who spend significant time studying God's Word during the interim to discern what God truly wants for the church—specifically, what God requires of a pastor. It may well help a number of persons to realize their expectations do not coincide with God's Word. This could bring about a time of spiritual revival and renewal within a congregation as they understand anew what God wishes and make sure they place their agenda in line with God's Word. Too many people place their own desires paramount when God's people should allow God's Word to be the driving force!

What Do We Need to Know?

For many years, my father-in-law has provided me with a complimentary subscription to the perennial American favorite magazine, *Reader's Digest*. One of the most popular features of the magazine is a section entitled "10 Things." It may be ten things that your doctor will not tell you, or your real estate agent, or your therapist, or your airline pilot. It is a popular section because it reveals the inner workings of the thoughts of those with whom we deal with on a regular basis. It is an exposé of things not publicly stated.

Many churches looking to hire a pastor, and many pastors looking to be hired, will go into the process not knowing how to find these otherwise hidden facts. There are many things that, simply put, search committees don't know they need to know! There is a deep need for honesty on the part of churches and candidates. To help assist in the encouragement of that honesty, this chapter forms what might be called the heart of this book. There are three sections of "10 Things" that I believe are extremely important. These issues go far beyond the pastor search process. They speak to the heart of the church and what happens in that group of persons who gather for worship, Bible study, and training.

These issues also speak to the often difficult-to-describe relationship between a pastor and a church. Having been a pastor for decades, I assure you that the relationship is special and unique. There is a bond that forms that can hardly be described in any other institution on earth. This is a bond of inexplicable tenderness. It is an intriguing bond. Sometimes, it is an incredibly painful bond. It certainly also contains the great possibility of providing an avenue by which God's kingdom is expanded. Thus, I share this chapter with you in great hopes that these issues will be understood, but also in great fear that they will not be understood. We are all human beings and see life through our own perspective. I pray that we will open our hearts and ask God to help us see from other perspectives, that together we might grow into a body of believers that is truly healthy.

10 Things a Pastor Wishes the Search Committee Had Revealed

When committees deal with ministers, a unique set of group dynamics is involved. We will deal more with this later. But for now we will look at one of the consequences of these unique dynamics. Having witnessed multiple search committee interactions over the past several decades, I can assure you that many ministers look back and wish that the following things had been revealed.

1. I wish the committee had revealed to me that they do not represent the church.

This is an issue that faces many ministers. While this may be something ministers wish had been revealed to them, people of maturity need to under-stand this reality from day one. The individuals who are selected to search for a new pastor are normally not the "rank and file" church members. While select-ing "average" church members does occur on occasion, often they are the most educated, astute, long-term members in the church. They are often elected because of their skill, popularity, or spiritual maturity. It is a terrible mistake for any minister to assume that the persons on the committee are indeed representative of the church and that the church is filled with people just like those whom you meet in an interview process.

2. I wish the committee had revealed that there were more problems than they let on.

I have heard this wish from countless ministers over the years. I receive calls regularly from pastors who are struggling in their settings, and invariably they say, "Why did they not tell me all the problems going on in the church?" I usually respond by explain-ing that, first of all, the committee probably did not know all of the problems, And second, if they had told you all of the problems, you would not have accepted the position! The DNA of every church is deeply complex and, like the DNA of human beings, is flawed in many regards. All churches have problems because churches are made up of human beings, and where there are human beings, there is an absolute certainty that problems are present. It is not a question of *if* or even a question of *when*. It is a question of *where*. Where do the problems truly lie? Many ministers naïvely believe they have been told all they need to know when they enter into a church situation. As I said earlier, sometimes the committee is simply unaware of the problems. They are not the pastor of the church and in most instances have not been the pastor of any church.

Many problems are private or unknown to search committee members. Therefore, candidates for a ministry job

> The DNA of every church is deeply complex.

must recognize clearly that only part of the story has been told. This is extremely important.

Perhaps this difficult situation might be assisted if the pastoral candidate asks some of the following questions:

- Is there someone who might be aware of internal issues in the church other than committee members? If so, please provide name and contact information.
- Have you heard of issues that you have not observed yourself but think might be present?
- What have people said who have left the church? Is there anyone aware of an exit interview or who has an understanding of why people have left the church?
- Would you mind if I spoke to the former pastor and asked if he was aware of situations I need to be aware of? What might he say?

3. I wish the committee realized they may be experts in their own vocation, but they are often unaware of what it takes to be a pastor.

This is an extremely crucial point and is at the heart of what causes problems in many, if not most, pastor search experiences. Let me share an illustration.

I once helped a church I previously pastored with their pastor search. I spoke with one of the committee members who was a vice president of a local bank. He is a dear soul who has been one of my greatest prayer supporters throughout my entire ministry. I love him dearly. In our interchange I said, "Let me ask you this question. When your bank needs a new president, do you think it would be wise for your bank to secure ten or twelve preachers to go out and find a new president for your bank?" He immediately responded that this was a ridiculous suggestion. I countered his retort with the following, "Why is that ridiculous? All of these pastors have had bank accounts for years. They have all spent much time in banks since they were young. Why would you not use them to search for your new president?" A smile came across his face, and he replied, "Point well taken!"

The truth is, many people who are gifted leaders in their own field of expertise, vocation, or field of study know little about what it takes to be a pastor. They think they know because they have served on committees, task forces, or teams, but they really do not know the innate leadership skills necessary to take people from point A to point B in a church setting.

If there is one thing I encourage churches to do, it is to seek the counsel of someone who has truly been a successful pastor. All pastor search committees or teams need to engage a company, a trusted pastor, or a denominational servant to assist them every step of the way. To neglect to secure counsel is to place the future of your church at great risk.

4. I wish I had been fully informed about the finances of the church.

Many pastors go to a church not knowing that the finances are in far worse shape than they imagined. While many churches or committees do provide a budget or even a finance report, there are many things they do not share. It could be that the committee itself does not know of serious problems that are present in the church's finances. Perhaps they have no idea that no true audit has been performed in years. Maybe they don't know of serious problems with cash flow. Many ministers come into a situation and are discouraged to find out that the church is in terrible financial shape. I once started a pastorate and was told within days that they barely had enough money to move my furniture

> To neglect to secure counsel is to place the future of your church at great risk.

to my new place of ministry. Things were in deep and serious trouble.

Most pastoral search committees send financial statements. However, those are often general and are not as revealing as some might wish. Few pastors are astute in accounting and business matters. Yet, one must ask for as much information as is readily available. Be sure to ask specific questions:

- What is the actual percentage of the church budget that goes to personnel matters? If it is over 50 percent, that is a huge red flag.
- How does the church handle designated accounts and designated giving? Ask for a list to review how many accounts exist and if they are used appropriately.
- Ask about the level of cash flow for the last year. Has the church been operating in the black or the red? Seasonal fluctuations occur, but you need to get a picture of what is happening financially.
- What is the debt of the church? What is the attitude of the church toward debt? For example, if the debt of the church is in excess of three times the annual budget, this is a major red flag. How

is the debt paid for? Who holds the note? Have the debt retirement payments been a problem for the church? What is the level of interest and the actual percentage being paid?

- How are financial decisions made? What process is present to guide financial decisions? What checks and balances are in place to guard against any possible incorrect usage of money?

Vanderbloemen is correct when he says churches experience a loss of momentum, decrease in attendance, and stagnant or decreased giving during the interim period.[6] While it would be unfair to expect the church's finances to be in a top-level position during the interim, it is still wise to ask for enough information to give a clear picture of where the church is at the time of the interview.

5. I wish the committee had told me that the last five pastors were asked to leave.

Some pastors share the following: No one actually told me that while there was no official church vote, a subgroup of people or an individual in the church had a hand in encouraging the previous ministers to vacate the office. Why was I not told this?

Again, everyone knew of these actions, but there may have been a point of embarrassment and fear that if this were revealed, the new pastor would not have come. Not only would this put the pastoral candidate in a position of fear for his job security, but it would reveal a serious pattern of disingenuousness or deceit.

In some churches, unfortunately, there are individuals who sense a pastor's popularity rising and fear their loss of power or influence. They begin to undermine the pastor and sometimes directly ask him to leave. A friend of mine was told a year into his first pastorate by a genuine friend that he only had six months left. When he inquired about this, he was told that a certain individual goes to every pastor about eighteen months in and asks him to leave. This was a case where the member felt his power threatened and sought to push almost every pastor out. My friend later confronted this church member and, in a somewhat humorous way, dealt with the situation. As some would say, he had a "come to Jesus" meeting with the man and remained at the church many years after that eighteen-month warning!

**6. I wish I had known that the pastor who died
was not actually perfect.**

On occasion, a pastor dies while still pastoring the
church. In many cases, this elevates this pastor to a
place likened to what might be called "sainthood." It
is very difficult for the new pastor to take that church
and change anything that may have been loved by the
former pastor—even if he was not a great pastor. Often
the faults, insecurities, and failures of the deceased
pastor are swept into the haze of history because of the
pastor's passing. People have a sort of selective nostal-
gia, forgetting about certain things and intentionally
leaving out others. The new pastor may be constantly
compared to the deceased and found lacking.

**7. I wish the committee had revealed that when
they said the church "had potential," they really
meant no one wanted to work.**

Virtually every search committee shares with a
prospective minister a series of statistical data points
that reveal the unreached population around the church,
the number of new housing developments within reach
of the church, and/or pockets of untapped ministry
potential within reach of the fellowship. While all of

that is good and needed, another question is often left unanswered: Why is this "unrealized potential" unrealized? Why are there such a large number of people who have not been witnessed to or ministered to? Every church has potential, but reality often points to a failure in the church's existence or past that reveals a lack of intentional ministry and evangelism. Many ministers are impressed with growth potential but fail to ask why that potential is still simply potential.

> Why is this "unrealized potential" unrealized?

8. I wish the committee had revealed that when they said the church wanted change, they really meant something different.

Invariably, many search committees are expressing what they wish to be true rather than that which is actually true. Many search committees are filled with visionary people who are elected to that position because of their leadership, sweet spirit, or longevity in the church membership. These members often do want the church to change and are astute enough to see the realities facing them. Perhaps they are aware of the decline or plateaued nature of the church and realize the need for change if the church is going to break through, transition, or grow once again. Just because they wish that or see that does not mean the church is willing or desirous of change. As we mentioned above, the search committee is often a skewed representation of the greater membership, and this is particularly true in conversations about change.

In my experience I have found many people who say they want change but quickly declare, "Pastor, please do not change the things I like." Change is hard for virtually every age group. We often attach this lack of desire for change to senior adults, but I have found that every age group can have a deep attachment to the status quo. In fact, students are often among those who most like things to stay the same. Resistance to change is a part of our human nature and condition.

9. I wish the committee had told me that the true power structure of the church does not always play fair.

As I teach young ministers, I teach them that one of the things they must do upon first arriving in a new fellowship is to discern whether or not the true power structure and the formal power structure align. Often there are persons of influence and power in the congregation who may not be in elected places of authority. Simply put, the real power brokers in the church may not always be those who are elected on the board as deacons or elders. Many ministers have come to learn that too late and wish they could have learned this beforehand.

10. I wish the committee had told me that their expectations were over-the-top.

Many ministers are deeply hurt when they recognize that the search team had rather high expectations, sometimes bordering on messianic expectations, of the new minister. Sadly that happens more often than not. There is a great deal of excitement when a new minister comes to a church. There are high expectations that things are going to happen to bring in many new people and help encourage the existing members. Those expectations are often abnormally high. Simply put, we cannot expect pastors—fallen men like the rest of us—to do things only Jesus can do.

I love the following illustration which, though humorous, speaks of our expectations.

"Superman" Staff Job Descriptions[7]

Pastor

Able to leap tall buildings in a single bound; more powerful than a locomotive; faster than a speeding bullet; walks on water; gives policies to God.

Associate Pastor

Able to leap short buildings in a single bound; as powerful as a switch engine; just as fast as a speeding bullet; walks on water if the sea is calm; talks with God.

Minister of Education

Leaps short buildings with a running start; almost as powerful as a switch engine; faster than a speeding BB; walks on water if he knows where the stumps are; talks with God if special request is approved.

Minister of Music

Clears a pup hut; loses race with a locomotive; can fire a speeding bullet; swims well; occasionally addressed by God.

Minister of Students

Runs into small buildings; recognizes locomotives two out of three times; used a squirt gun in college;

knows how to use the water fountain; mumbles to himself.

Church Secretary/Ministry Assistant

Lifts buildings to walk under them; kicks locomotives off the tracks; catches speeding bullets in her teeth; freezes water with a single glance; when God speaks, she says, "May I ask who's calling?"

Obviously, this humorous illustration speaks of the varying degrees of expectation for staff members. However, as humorous as the "Superman" job description given to the pastor may be, I have found in many instances the level of expectation is abnormally high. Be careful not to hold your new pastor to a standard which is more than any human being could attain.

10 Things Churches Wish Their Former Pastor Had Told Them

1. We wish he had told us he was struggling with burnout.

Many pastors fail to reveal to their congregations and even to the leaders in the congregation that they struggle in various areas. One area in which pastors struggle is the constant, looming threat of burnout. Statistics are not certain about the number of pastors who leave the ministry due to burnout, but they are too high, to say the least.

Every week several pastors of evangelical and Southern Baptist churches leave the ministry due to burnout. This reality occurs due to a large number of factors, circumstances, and events. Sometimes there are undue expectations. Sometimes the level of emotion required to deal with domestic situations, counseling, staff leadership, and difficult church members simply takes a toll on pastors. The emotional drain allows no time or opportunity to be "recharged."

Some pastors struggle with burnout and do not realize the symptoms or the encroaching effects of it upon their lives, family, and, most importantly, their spiritual walk. Some years ago, Bill Hybels wrote an article in *Christianity Today* about burnout and accurately relayed the fact that many pastors deal greatly with "IMAs–Intensive Ministry Activities." I have referred to these as "emotionally draining activities" or EDAs, which are often accompanied with EDPs or "emotionally draining people."[8] Obviously, people deal with those situations in every area of life and in every business and commercial venture. However, the pastor is asked to deal with these situations at a higher level and in a more protracted manner than others. While Hybels and others wisely advise that we should limit our exposure to EDAs and EDPs, sometimes it is simply not possible in the pastorate. Many pastors struggle and do not understand the warning signs of impending burnout.

I recently spoke in a very small church where the pastor was refreshingly honest. He told me this was his first church after a twelve-year burnout season. He confessed that he had allowed his personal devotional time to suffer during his earlier ministry. Because he was not being refueled by a daily, intimate time with the Lord and God's Word, he began to burn out and experience a long hiatus in the ministry. It was refreshing to hear someone talk honestly and openly about this subject. Fortunately, he also shared this with his congregation and they are deeply respectful of his personal journey and honesty.

2. We wish he had told us he felt a lack of support.

Many pastors, as discussed in the first instance of struggling with burnout, simply refuse to complain. In their efforts not to heap their problems on others, they refuse to reveal their negative feelings about certain situations. Others simply refuse to be transparent about these things because they feel somehow that it might reveal some weakness on their part, and they certainly do not desire to reveal that! While pastors refuse to share these needs for a variety of reasons, the results inevitably produce more bad than good.

It is true that in every pastorate there are individuals who are looking for the pastor's weaknesses. Sometimes when a weakness is revealed, and it is a possible glaring weakness, it almost seems to excite and enliven certain persons. This is an unfortunate truth. We are living in a time when leadership is looked upon not with a great respect but with a certain cynicism and distrust. Many ministers feel a lack of support and know that the support they have might be short-lived.

Similar to marriages, new pastors and their churches often experience a "honeymoon phase" for the first few weeks or even months. There is a period of grace extended for a new minister as he learns situations, develops strategies, and implements his new vision. Wise ministers take their time in implementing massive change. But, a time of favor is often given to new ministers because of their greenness. Many wise ministers know that time will end at some point.

Like all humans, pastors deeply need unconditional love from their friends. They need to know that there are people who have their backs. And while these friends will certainly share constructive criticism, they need to know that there are people who will stand with them through the good and the bad, the easy and the hard.

Certainly, individuals who are part of a pastor search team or committee should form a support group for the pastor, whether formal or informal. Hopefully, the relationship with the new pastor will be an ongoing one of unconditional love and support. Again, honest, instructive criticism should be an expected part of this relationship, but there must also be an unconditional acceptance and love that is profound.

3. We wish he had told us that he felt insecure in several areas.

In the twenty-first century church—because of technology and the proliferation of experts and accomplished practitioners constantly thrust before us in books, websites, and more—the average, normal pastor has feelings of insecurity. He feels he cannot match the preaching, writing, and expertise exhibited by some of these national authorities. The fact that church members have instant access to these preaching and writing giants breeds insecurity on the part of many pastors. There are days when pastors want to stand up and shout, "I'm just a man!" And, yes, I am just an ordinary man. I cannot match the preaching of Adrian Rogers! I cannot equal the intellect of David Dockery or Al Mohler! I cannot match the writing skills of Tim Keller or Charles Colson! I cannot match the leadership skills of Henry Blackaby or John Maxwell.

> These are days when pastors want to stand up and shout, "I'm just a man!"

This insecurity leaves many pastors feeling terribly alone. In spite of the fact that they are deluged with daily activities and meetings, they often feel alone and terribly misunderstood.

4. We wish he had told us that he could never "rest in the call" because he didn't have one.

The concept of a call from God outlined in 1 Samuel 3 about the prophet Samuel is foreign to many in the twenty-first-century church. Every pastor should have a clear calling from God not only to ministry but also to the specific place where God has placed him. This ability to confirm a word of direction from God should also result in a lifestyle of "resting in the call." It gives a person great confidence when he knows he is where he is by the hand of God. Sadly, many in today's culture do not understand this and often go with emotions or logic to determine their place of ministry or current vocation. This leads to great instability and, unfortunately, to the minister's questioning his call or even leaving at the first sign of difficulty.

One of the most important things for a search team or committee to hear from a pastoral candidate is clarity of the call. Can this person clearly verbalize his call to the ministry? Ask the candidate to share it clearly and in detail. Also, ask if he has experienced a calling from the Lord to that particular church? How has he sensed this call? How has this been evidenced? Has his wife also sensed this calling? At what point did he believe this calling became clear? These are vital questions to ask in order to discern God's direction in the candidate's life and also the certainty of call to that place.

I am well aware that the concept of sensing a call from God may seem somewhat mystical and subjective. We often attach God's name to our own personal agendas. I have counseled many people over the years regarding this issue.

That does not mean, however, that we should not seek clarity. In all honesty, sometimes the call is as clear as day. Often the call is given through scriptural admonition, and the person recognizes that the Lord was speaking through that Scripture passage to them. Other times this clarity of call comes from a long period of prayer in which a "simple peace" comes upon a person, and they know the direction they should go. Sometimes the call comes through the affirmation of many other believers who also have the Holy Spirit. A few people even claim to hear audible words from God! Whatever the situation may be and however God speaks to a person, we must seek affirmation from our Lord when something as important as going to a new church is the issue.

5. We wish he had told us his wife hated ministry.

Unfortunately, in many situations one's spouse may become a major factor in ministry success or failure. Often the wife does not feel the same sense of calling her husband does. Often the personality of the spouse may indeed impinge upon the leadership of the pastor. There are multiple examples of a spouse becoming so aggressively involved in leadership that the church does not know who the true pastor is! I cannot tell you the number of times churches have dealt with this issue, and almost always the resulting damage is catastrophic. Many churches so wish they had known the personality of the spouse and the ability of the called pastor to lead without harmful influence from his wife.

With that being said, many spouses, even those who are not aggressive in personality or those who have a sense of calling, still can become bitter if they feel the church has failed to guard the pastor. Many pastors bring their work home and, regrettably, can be a part of building bitterness on the part of the spouse or even on the part of the children. The family begins to see the church as a competitor for their time and affection. Unfortunately, they begin to hear some of the "underbelly" of church politics and can become embittered at the church and, sadly, can carry over that bitterness toward the Lord.

Moreover, pastors' wives often fail to be cared for by the church. They do not feel they have the freedom to join a small group and confess sins, fears, or weaknesses because, as the pastor's wife, they are supposed to be "above that." Ironically, many pastors' wives feel completely isolated and alienated from healthy Christian community.

This calls for maturity on the part of the pastor to guard the heart of his family and be careful how much and what he shares from his daily work at the church. While desirous of transparency, pastors need to learn that they do not need to share everything. A pastor neither needs to share every detail of the church with his wife, nor does he need to share every detail about his wife with the church! Every minister also needs to realize the calling of God needs to be for the entire family, if at all possible. With that said, the pastor is the leader and needs be seen as the leader.

Many pastors' families wish the church better understood boundaries and appropriate demand for time and attention. They simply want a church to guard the family so that there may be nurture, growth, and protection of the pastor's family.

> Many pastors' families wish the church better understood boundaries.

6. We wish he had told us he does not know how to handle conflict.

I have often shared in seminars that the difference between a good pastor and a great pastor is the ability to handle conflict biblically, appropriately, and effectively. Many churches do not know how to handle conflict, and, regrettably, this has been taught to them by their leaders. In all circles, evangelical and non-evangelical, the issue of how to handle conflict is of crucial importance. Many pastors simply do not have the experience or skills to handle it.

Many people, including pastors, avoid or run from conflict, thus making it worse. Others blunder into conflict not knowing how to handle it appropriately. The result is a continuing and deepening festering of agendas, disagreements, and hurt feelings, and often a departure from the church or something even worse. The "even worse" occurs when various groups become solidified in their opposition to one another and often to the leadership of the church. While almost no one likes conflict, churches desperately need leaders who know how to handle conflict in an appropriate and constructive manner.

For example, does the pastor follow Matthew 18 and encourage, if not require, all church leaders to use this biblical strategy? Is conflict handled in a timely manner, or is it postponed until issues become "holy wars"? Do the church and the pastor recognize the reality of spiritual warfare and how it is energized in the arena of conflict?

It is important for a church to understand the necessity of church discipline. While this book is not the place for a full discussion of this issue, I have found many churches lacking in their understanding of church discipline and often unwilling to take church discipline to the full extent of biblical instruction and command.

Ask yourself this question: Will we support our new pastor if he truly seeks to enforce Matthew 18? Will our deacons as well as all of our church leaders follow Matthew 18? These are important issues. I have often said that the difference between good and great churches is the ability to handle conflict and do so in a way that honors our Lord. Matthew 18 is not just a nice thing to do; it is an imperative. God's instructions in Matthew 18 work not only for the church, but they also work in the family and the business world. Businessmen and women could see their businesses transformed if the Matthew 18 principles about interpersonal conflict were followed even in the business world.

7. We wish he had told us that when he arrived he was already looking for another place to go.

Unfortunately, the "ladder-climbing pastor" is very much a part of evangelical circles. In many instances, the call of God is part of a process of always looking for something bigger and better, something offering more money and more influence. Ambition is an issue of discussion that causes many in the

Christian world to be nervous. Is it wrong for a pastor to be ambitious? What are the limits to that ambition? Should there be transparency about this?

These questions need to be asked. Churches are deeply hurt when the pastor moves on quickly, and they wonder if he ever settled down or thought of the place as home.

This is an issue pastors need to resolve in their lives. I have known pastors who were talking about their next place of ministry within months of their arrival at their new place of "calling." There seems to be, on the part of some ministers, an intentional strategy to use churches as merely stepping-stones toward something greater, bigger, and more prestigious.

This has been encouraged in recent years by the hiring of young, often inexperienced persons in churches of prominence. On rare occasion this works well; however, it usually ends badly. Seeing those rare instances that have worked well only serves to increase the belief on the part of many inexperienced persons that they too should be moving up far more rapidly than seems to be happening in their lives.

While a search committee can wish for transparency and honesty, they must be diligent in looking at the track record of each candidate to see how often he has moved and why he moved when he did.

8. We wish he had told us that his claims to be overworked were not actually true.

Often, the claims of overworked conditions among ministers are a smoke screen for poor time management skills and, on occasion, for laziness. Pastors and ministers do have demands that are easily verifiable and true in almost every situation. Yet, pastors who become successful learn to delegate and prioritize. Some pastors simply do not know how to do so. As a result, their lives become complicated with competing demands, and they are overwhelmed when they try to do everything. Others simply stretch out certain tasks far longer than is necessary in order to perpetuate the myth of the overworked pastor, and, on occasion, they excuse their own laziness.

One unfortunate truth about many ministers is their insecurity regarding delegation. There is insecurity on the part of ministers that feel they are the only ones who can accomplish a task, and they have failed to remember the biblical job description that was cited earlier in this book. They forget that their job is to train and to delegate, so that the ministry will expand far beyond their own ability and not to do all the ministry on their own. This lack of confidence has hurt the ministry of many pastors and churches.

This is a hard word and will offend some, but having worked with pastors for decades, I can assure you that these scenarios are often true. Many denominations post the average number of hours worked by the clergy. They are often quite extreme. Yes, some work that long and that hard. There are some congregations and locations that demand more than others.

The pastors in our evangelical framework for whom I have the most respect are the bi-vocational pastors who often work a full-time job in order to do ministry, and often the ministry position is full-time as well. These men are the true heroes of the faith! They juggle work, ministry, and family in a way that is truly exceptional. Thus, when I hear other pastors complain about being overworked, I have little sympathy.

By the way, statistically bi-vocational pastors make up the majority of evangelical churches in our country. In fact, in many states the number of bi-vocational pastors is as high as 80 percent. Many people expect bi-vocational pastors to be the norm in the future, as many churches are moving to multiple ministers in preaching, ministering, and other roles, and expect their ministers to be bi-vocational or professional in another vocation, as well as lead in ministry.

9. We wish he had told us that he had specific theological leanings, which we definitely needed to know.

There was another day and time where the big argument in evangelical circles was whether one identified with a premillennialist, postmillennialist, or amillennialist view in their understanding of the end times. Long and great discussions occurred concerning one's positions about eschatology. While there still may be some who debate these issues, today other issues are far more argued and discussed.

In many evangelical circles, people still wonder about one's belief in the inspiration of Scripture. Does one hold to a view of inerrancy or infallibility? Does one hold to a verbal, plenary view of inspiration or a dynamic view of inspiration? How does one view certain parts of Scripture? Does one believe that the Scripture contains truth or is truth? These and a variety of other questions, which we will review later, help identify where a person is in this particular area. Many churches, however, end up wishing they had known how their pastor felt about Scripture prior to his being hired.

Additionally, in evangelical circles today, the issue of Calvinism and non-Calvinism is perhaps the hottest topic among pastor search committees dealing with the issue of soteriology. Calvinists and non-Calvinists have had an uneasy coexistence in evangelical circles for many years.

Some readers may ask, "What is Calvinism?" It is amazing the number of persons in our churches who are unaware of this particular view of soteriology, the study of salvation. Much has been written about this subject, including a book I wrote many years ago entitled *Trouble with the TULIP*. There is not time or space in this book to discuss this subject. However, it is a belief held by Presbyterians and many other evangelicals, particularly of the younger demographic, who believe in five points about the doctrine of salvation espoused by the followers of John Calvin, which form the acrostic T-U-L-I-P. The five points are:

T = Total depravity

U = Unconditional election

L = Limited atonement

I = Irresistible grace

P = Perseverance of the saints

The issues primarily revolve around the doctrines represented in the middle three points dealing with the question of whether or not God predestined some to eternal life and some to damnation, and whether or not Christ's atonement was limited only for the elect (or chosen), or if it was for everyone.

There is presently a growing movement of Calvinistic pastors in evangelical churches and in Southern Baptist churches. Look at the following statistics:

- In polling SBC pastors, LifeWay Research found that "sixty-six percent of pastors do not consider their church a reformed theology congregation, while 30 percent agree (somewhat strongly) with the statement 'My church is theologically Reformed or Calvinist.' Four percent did not know."

- In addition, when SBC pastors were asked whether or they are "concerned about the impact of Calvinism in our convention," 35 percent strongly agreed, and 26 percent somewhat agreed. Only 16 percent strongly disagreed, and 14 percent somewhat disagreed.[9]

Clearly the issue is growing in evangelical circles and certainly in Southern Baptist churches. Dr. Paige Patterson, president of Southwestern Baptist Theological Seminary, has said repeatedly that many of our problems would go away if there were total honesty up front. Churches need to be clear about where they stand regarding the issues of reformed theology, and they need to share those concerns and beliefs with all ministerial candidates. Equally important is the need for pastoral candidates to be extremely open and honest with churches, teams, and committees concerning their belief about reformed or Calvinistic theology. While churches and ministers can change and grow, not to reveal these leanings is simply disingenuous. Churches want to know where their pastor stands in these areas as well as others.

10. We wish he had told us that when the church grew, it outgrew his skills.

One of the big issues churches face is the issue of competency. One wise, older pastor told me many years ago when I was pastoring a church that was growing at a fast rate that "when the church doubles, one-half of the staff members will become incompetent." I have thought about that statement quite a bit over the years and have found it to be absolutely true. Certain staff members and pastors can work well in a setting of a certain size but are not as equipped to handle all the spinning plates that come with a large church.

Let me say it this way—some ministers are doers, while others are managers. In other words, some people know how to delegate and train people in works of ministry, while others believe their job is to do everything and be involved in every aspect of ministry. Those persons in the latter category struggle and become frustrated as a situation grows and they find they cannot keep their hands in every situation.

There are wonderful pastors who are great leaders at certain levels of church growth, but they end up in over their head at other levels. Churches wish they had known this and might have provided extra assistance or training for their minister. Often pastors and ministers fail to recognize this reality and to

> Some ministers are doers, while others are managers.

admit their shortcomings. Happy is the church who has a pastor who understands who he is and who he is not!

10 Things the Candidate Will Not Tell the Committee

1. The candidate will not tell the committee his weaknesses.

It is obligatory to ask a candidate about his weaknesses, and every search committee does. But the truth is, you will rarely hear an honest answer. Sometimes the pastoral candidate does not know his weaknesses. Perhaps he has been told what they are but doesn't really believe it. Most often the candidate might answer, "I am not patient" or "I struggle with mediocrity." Rarely will the committee see the transparency of a person who tells you things that are embarrassing or downright demeaning about his own character or personality.

A pastor search committee needs to pay close attention to issues that surface during the search process. Though these issues may seem small or insignificant, they may become major later on. For example, if a candidate does not return phone calls regularly in the search process, this could indicate a propensity that might prove very damaging later in his ministry. Another example is a lack of decisiveness. While many issues call for great prayer and discernment, if a candidate is seemingly unable to make decisions during the search team process, this may be indicative of a lack of ability to make decisions and lead in a strong way in the days ahead.

In other words, do not ignore the small things during the search process, as they can become big things!

2. The candidate will not tell the committee of his failures in ministry.

Only on rare occasions will the committee have a candidate who shares of times where he has failed to exercise good judgment or leadership in ministry. Most teams or committees know this must be discovered through a search of references and those who may know the candidate from the past.

I often say, in a teasing manner, that if you really want to know inside information about a person, you need to contact the church secretary or administrative assistant where the candidate served previously. Believe me, the administrative assistant always knows! Often, however, ministry assistants or secretaries will not divulge any information. Again, one must be persistent! Asking another administrative assistant to call that assistant may well yield much-needed

> The administrative assistant always knows!

information. Though it may seem awkward at times, you will sleep well at night knowing you did your best to avoid hiring a candidate with too many deep, dark secrets from his past.

3. The candidate will not tell the committee that he does not have twenty years of experience.

The candidate's résumé may show twenty years of experience, but he will not tell you that he actually has five years of experience that he repeated four times, or even worse, two years of experience that he repeated ten times. Many people only learn so much, and then they repeat that experience or learning multiple times. Few will be honest about this.

4. The candidate will not tell the committee that his personality type may not fit the church.

I once connected with a church through encouraging them in the work of missions and ministries. I found the pastor to be open about the reality that his personality type did not fit his current job description. It was giving him great difficulty, and as a result, he believed the church was not doing as well as it could because of his personality style. It is incumbent upon every team or committee to do an analysis, perhaps even professionally, of the candidate's personality type to make sure he will be a fit for the church.

5. The candidate will not tell the committee that he learned his interview skills from a website or seminar.

The candidate will certainly not tell you that his interview skills do not match his day-to-day performance. This is, however, often the case. I have seen situations where a person interviewed so well that the committee thought they were getting the greatest minister ever for that position. Yet, in subsequence reference checks, the reality of day-to-day performance came nowhere close to the interview skill presented.

6. The candidate will not tell the committee he is climbing a career ladder.

No candidate is going to reveal to the committee that the church is simply a stepping-stone to something greater in his grand scheme of personal kingdom building. Again that may sound harsh, but many see a church only as one step in a grander scheme. As we have reviewed already, ambition needs to be discussed. It is not necessarily negative, but it must be seen as a part of God's inner working in a person's life to make himself better in one sense and also to use the skills God has given him in the greatest way.

7. The candidate will not tell the committee that he may have already moved in his heart to your church, and not hearing from the committee deeply hurts.

This happens numerous times as ministers who are being dealt with by a committee or team become deeply, emotionally vested in the church. Please be kind enough to keep them informed as to the committee's progress, and let them know if and when you are no longer considering them. The call of the church is to be gracious and compassionate to all, and leaving a pastoral candidate hanging as to his status is no way to show grace or compassion.

8. The candidate will not tell the committee that the letters urging you to consider him are from him.

Often, letters are sent to a committee or church encouraging them to consider a certain person, but these letters are encouraged by the candidate himself. While you may want to believe it is because of his overwhelming demonstration of leadership, it may be that he is networking the system to encourage further consideration from you. The candidate will rarely share that he desperately needs to leave where he is and, therefore, has orchestrated a letter campaign.

9. The candidate will not tell the committee that the sermons you have heard are good but are not typical.

Please consider this point well. The committee must ensure due diligence and thoroughly investigate the candidate's preaching and teaching ability. Every pastor can create a few good sermons; however, the committee must research and consider the long-term preaching and teaching ability of the candidate. Preachers used to refer to these best sermons as "sugar sticks." They were finely honed and well-practiced sermons that were used often in revivals and other settings. The committee needs to listen and review many sermons to see the overall quality of a candidate's messages and preaching style.

Another issue that is extremely disturbing but also important to know is that a number of preachers preach other people's sermons. Countless pastors have gotten into trouble by using another's messages much too literally. Churches have fired their pastor when they found out he was preaching verbatim an Adrian Rogers or a Jerry Vines sermon. At times, the pastors would use the illustrations as if they had occurred to them personally.

Please, take note of this. Every preacher uses material from other pastors, commentaries, and other sources. That is acceptable. However, a pastor needs to make the sermon his own! If he quotes another person, he must adequately reference that person. Listen carefully to the sermons to see if they are consistent with the style and personality of that pastor or minister.

Another point that must be understood is that if a candidate preaches for an hour and is informed that this will not work in the current situation and he agrees to preach thirty minutes, then eventually he will defer back to the one-hour time frame. I have seen this occur repeatedly as preachers who like to preach an extended length agree to a shorter message, teaching, or sermon time in order to please a team or committee, only to revert back to their lengthier, preferred time of presentation.

10. The candidate will not tell the committee he is actually dealing with multiple churches at the same time.

Often teams or committees are dealing with three candidates at one time. But you may not know that the candidate is doing the same thing. Yes, this is a question that needs to be asked, and it is something that both committee and candidate need to avoid. While it is appropriate to interview several persons

> The pastor desperately needs to deal seriously with only one church at a time.

at once, when a committee becomes seriously interested, it needs to deal with one candidate at a time. The pastor desperately needs to deal seriously with only one church at a time. This is an extremely important principle.

Many lives are at stake. Serious prayer and consideration of one situation at a time will prevent confusion and broken hearts. Please, be honest with all parties.

What Should We Avoid?

 While there will be a specific chapter later regarding how to get started, I believe it is important at this time to outline several strategies that many pastor search teams and committees employ—most of which need to be avoided assiduously. Some of these strategies have been employed commonly in the past, some are currently used, and others are being seen as the new way to select pastors. Regardless, for the most part, these are unhelpful strategies that I encourage you to avoid as you go about this important task.

The Horse-Race Strategy

This strategy was once a common practice. It consisted of committees inviting several preachers and allowing them to preach on a given Sunday, one after another, for several weeks. Many years ago, I had a visit from a church that I will never forget. They had identified me as one of their probable candidates and asked for me to preach as part of a month-long competition. The church would vote, and the one with the highest number of votes at the end of the month would get the job. I cannot think of a worse strategy. It ignores those very important factors, beyond preaching, that make a pastor a great pastor.

This kind of strategy may seem democratic, but it is dangerous. It is similar to the "annual call" that many churches formerly used. In these churches the pastor's job was secure for only one year. After that, he had to have another vote of confidence, in essence, from the congregation. Again, this is a seemingly democratic practice, but it leads to a serious denial of the authority of the pastor and of his place as the leader of the church.

By the way, I declined the offer to preach at that church and am so thankful that I did.

The Play-It-Safe Strategy

This might also be called "The Safety Move." I see a number of churches employ this strategy in their pastor search process. Often, this strategy is played out by the hiring of a former staff member or a current staff member. Employing the "we know him" factor, these churches cater to the need for safety and comfort among members. On occasion, this works and works well. However, I can point to a larger number of churches who have gone this direction and have begun immediately to decline, never being able to pull back out of that decision. As we will discuss later, one of the key issues here is the failure to recognize that just because a person has skills in one area does not mean those skills are transferrable to another level of leadership. Sometimes they are, but often a person who may be an exemplary youth pastor is not capable of leading the church as the senior pastor. Simply because people trust someone or people like someone does not give that person the ability to lead a church to grow, thrive, and be a serious success. I have seen this approach succeed in few churches, but in almost every instance it comes back to bite the committee as they have played the safety factor when they should have been looking for the best new leader for the church.

The Risk-It-All Strategy

This "go for broke" strategy is one that is being used increasingly across our nation. In this kind of strategy, the search team or committee recommends or hires a person who is totally untried in that position. I can personally think of only two examples across our nation where churches brought in a person who had no experience as a senior pastor and saw this strategy succeed in a beautiful way. One of these examples includes a pastor, having never been a senior pastor before, taking the church to levels it never even dreamed. He is a truly humble, godly man who has honored the DNA of the church as well as the former pastor who retired. In his humility and dependence on the Lord, he has also exhibited powerful and exemplary leadership skills.

I cannot even begin to share the number of churches who have used this strategy and have risked the future of the church only to find that the risk was not worth taking. Church after church across the nation has employed someone

no experience and has seen the ch

numbers, effectiveness, finances, miss

and more. Oftentimes committees naïvel

because they have hired someone who has s

larger church staff, the person is capable of 1

large or megachurch. Again, rarely does that ha

Let me use a secular illustration. There are n

bers of championship, college-level coaches who ha

been some of the greatest coaches in history but hav

failed at the professional (NFL) level. Why is this? I

believe skill sets are needed at one level that may not

be present in a person at a

different setting or level.

To think that because one

has been a successful staff

member, and therefore is

capable of leading a

church, is a serious mis-

> This "risk it all" factor is a decision that must be avoided.

judgment. This "risk it all" factor is a decision that

must be avoided. Please heed this warning!

e Know-It-All Strategy

This is employed across our nation. Many committees feel that they are capable of finding a pastor because, after all, "being a pastor is not all that hard." Many members on pastor search committees think they know all they need to know because "being a pastor is like being a leader in any other field." In other words, the skills necessary to succeed in one vocation will work in another vocation because those skills can be replicated or transferred.

Please heed this warning. As I have pointed out, committees need to understand the uniqueness of pastoring. They also must understand that churches need pastors of varying skill sets for the various church sizes. Some pastors would be a great fit for a small church but would be overwhelmed in a megachurch. Likewise, some pastors would be a great fit in a megachurch but would not have the skill set to shepherd a small church.

> Committees need to understand the uniqueness of pastoring.

I cannot overestimate this point. Just as business people know that running a small business is dramatically different from being a CEO of a large national or international corporation, people need to understand that similar forces are at work in the church world. Just because one has been a successful pastor of a church that runs a membership of three hundred does not mean he is capable of running a church of two thousand. He may well be! However, there is a necessary skill set and experience level that is appropriate for certain sizes of churches. This is why a church committee needs to involve a trusted advisor to help discern the skill levels of pastoral candidates.

Every vocation is unique. While some leadership characteristics are true for all vocations and situations, pastors are unique in their vocation. A church needs to be careful to do its due diligence and study carefully what it takes to pastor a church and what skill sets that particular church might need. Only when this is done can a church hire a man who has the calling and gifting necessary to be a pastor and who has the right skill set for their specific church.

The Failure-to-(Almost)-Launch Strategy

There are situations when the people recognize that the church has gone through a difficult time and needs to heal before the church hires a new pastor. We know that Satan is at work. We know the church is hurting. We know that there are things that can be done during an interim to bring healing and refocus to a church. However, a church needs a leader, and the members usually expect that the leader is the lead or senior pastor. If a hurting church is left to heal without a senior pastor, the healing process might not go smoothly. In other words, don't wait too long.

Again, we will deal with this later as we discuss the issue of an interim or transitional pastor, but please know that interim and transitional pastors can be extremely helpful to assist a church in healing. It is rare, however, for a church to experience growth or even stasis during an interim time. In almost every instance, people who are looking to join a church wait until the new pastor comes. Also, when a church does not have a permanent senior pastor, forces of disunity begin to mount within the fellowship. The longer the church goes without a permanent leader, the more likely those forces of disunity will come to the forefront. Yes, please pray, but also act to make sure the church gets a leader as soon as possible.

The Replication Strategy

This is a variation of the "Play-It-Safe Strategy." In other words, many churches insist on searching for a pastor who is just like the last one. He did a good job, so let's get a pastor just like him. While that may or may not be wise, it often ignores the fact that churches may have changed and the skill set needed may now be different. Has the church grown? Has the church declined? Is the church in a major crisis? Perhaps the skill set needed in the new pastor is not like the skill set of the former pastor. It is extremely important that churches do an analysis of where they are and what the needs might be in this current experience.

> Churches may have changed and the skill set needed may now be different.

The Let-the-Pastor-Choose-His-Successor Strategy

This is a strategy used in many large churches and sometimes even in smaller churches where there has been a trusted, long-term leader. Unfortunately some pastors begin to think the church is theirs, and it is their right to name their successor. Other churches use family members or a son to take up the mantle and continue the father's leadership.

When there has been a long-term, successful pastor, many people are concerned about the succession of leadership. People wondered what would happen when Jerry Falwell died in 2007. Many predicted that the church and university he founded would decline or die. Today, both the church and university have seen growth that they never saw under the leadership of Jerry Falwell.

Conversely, I can also point out numerous examples of churches that had long-term, successful pastors who will never see those glory days again. The succession plan simply did not work. In an article by Warren Bird in *Christianity Today* on November 18, 2014, he talks about this leadership succession issue. In this article, Bird quotes Linda Stanley, vice president and team leader for Leadership Network. "The large-church pastors . . . ages 45 to 65," Stanley said, "may talk about succession. But few if any have actually detailed a plan."

Bird also points out that many churches are using the "Family Plan," where a long-term pastor hands the leadership of the church over to a son or daughter. Crystal Cathedral's Robert Schuller attempted to do this, and since then the church has dissolved and disbanded. Again, Jerry Falwell accomplished this with great success, but his case seems to be the exception rather than the rule. Bird also talks about the "Denominational Plan." This strategy works when there is some type of hierarchical structure whereby the denomination can assist in finding a successor or new pastor. This is not true in most evangelical and Baptist settings.

In addition, Bird details the "Process-Only Plan." In this plan, the departing pastor assists in creating and implementing a succession plan and then leaves. This kind of process happened at First Baptist Orlando where Pastor Jim Henry set into motion a succession plan and, within months of the new pastor's arrival, exited the setting. The church has experienced great success.

Finally, Bird talks about the "Intentional Overlap Plan" where large-church pastors intentionally overlap the successor. I can tell you from experience that this seldom works. On occasion, the pastor simply cannot let go of leadership, or the church itself cannot follow the new leader.

On rare occasions, however, this kind of strategy works well. A trusted, long-term pastor, whether the church is large or small, intentionally and sequentially turns over more and more of the leadership to the new, chosen pastor. This can be an extremely successful strategy, but it also holds great risks. The egos of both of the leaders must be held in check. One of the great stories of success in this regard is Southeast Christian Church in Louisville, Kentucky. The long-term, successful pastor was able to transition the church to the new leader, and after some initial decline the church began to see great growth.

It is so important when discerning the DNA of a church to see how that DNA matches not only with the potential candidate for pastor or minister but with the plan to install the new pastor or minister.

I have seen a well-known church in one of the southern states dramatically decline over the last several years because they called a pastor who is a bad fit. I shared my concerns with a staff member immediately when hearing of this person being named as pastor of that church. The man happened to be a friend, a man I respect and love. The church is one I know and love. I had known the former pastor of the church. While I loved both the church and the pastor, I knew it was a "round peg in a square hole" kind of situation. The preaching style, length, and leadership style were dramatically different from the former pastor. I knew the church well enough to know that this different style of leadership and preaching would not fit. Now the church has reached a point so low that it may never be able to recover, even if new leadership were to come into place.

It is extremely important not only to discern the DNA of the church but also that of the candidate and make sure it is a good fit.

Question 4

Do We Need an Interim?

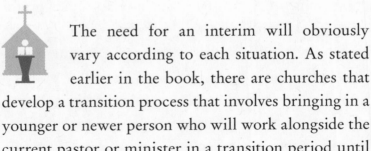 The need for an interim will obviously vary according to each situation. As stated earlier in the book, there are churches that develop a transition process that involves bringing in a younger or newer person who will work alongside the current pastor or minister in a transition period until the newer person is ready to assume the job duties. In these occasions, the former or current minister begins to reduce his responsibilities, change to a different role, or remove himself altogether. In those cases, there is no need for any kind of interim assistance in its traditionally known fashion.

However, the vast majority of churches still use some kind of committee or team search process that does not involve the pastor slowly handing off responsibility, and in those instances the church needs to use the services of an interim.

Rotating Staff as Preachers

Remember question 3, "What Should We Avoid?" That chapter included a warning about bringing in a candidate or possible pastor who had been successful in some other ministry but had no senior pastor experience. Remember this warning when a church seeks to use staff members during the interim time to replace the senior pastor. While the factor of trust and knowing an individual seems to be overwhelming, the fact that those persons are not in a senior pastor position is often because they are not qualified to do so. While it is different for an interim, there are many reasons why this kind of scenario can be, but is not always, counterproductive. What are some of those?

First of all, if a church chooses to use staff members during the interim time, it must be clear that they cannot ever be considered to be the senior pastor.

Invariably certain staff members do seek that position and often will begin to develop a series of communications and support systems to encourage the committee to consider them. If that person is regularly in the pulpit, this only exacerbates the issue. An "us versus them" mentality begins to develop among various parts of the congregation. Staff members may begin to try and compete against other staff members. In virtually every place where a church uses a series of staff members to preach during an interim time, this kind of disunity rises and attendance falls. Please listen carefully to this warning.

> An "us versus them" mentality begins to develop.

On rare occasions, it does work. While the staff will often continue the day-to-day ministry of a church, rarely can the health of the church withstand the lack of consistency in the pulpit.

Outside Interim

In most occasions a church needs an outside interim to assist during the interim process. What are the advantages to this? First of all, it provides stability in the pulpit. In our twenty-first-century world, most people who come to a church or even consider a church often see the pulpit ministry as a key place of connection. We all know that there is a core group of people who will come virtually every Sunday no matter who is in the pulpit. However, there is a large number of people who are not so committed and find themselves drifting from consistency when there is no stability in the pulpit.

Many churches also find themselves having to deal with some crucial issues during an interim time period. Often when the previous pastor has left in a less than positive way, there are issues of disunity, distrust, hurt, and grief taking place in the congregation. Even in the best of circumstances, the grief is real, and there needs to be time for the healing of that grief and processing of those emotions before a congregation is ready for a new pastor.

Therefore, I encourage churches to seriously consider an interim pastor who is trustworthy and who is not seeking the job for himself! This ought to be the first question that is asked of every interim. It is important in most cases to communicate clearly up front that the interim prospect will not be considered for a full-time ministry position. If he is, some of the same issues mentioned above regarding the staff can be present. One of the primary reasons this is difficult is because it short-circuits the work of the committee. The person who is preaching every Sunday is already developing relationships and perhaps will not get the same scrutiny as other candidates. There are certainly rare exceptions to this probability, and there have been some wonderful interims who became full-time pastors and ministers that have succeeded. However, there are dozens of examples of failure in this regard as well.

The role of interim, sometimes called transitional pastor, can be significant in helping a church deal with issues before a new minister or pastor is called. Many Baptist state conventions now offer training courses for pastors to become specifically transitional pastors. This is a pastor who comes in with a specific job assignment. He has skills in conflict resolution and vision casting and can help a church deal with issues during the interim so they will be ready when the new pastor comes to take the church to an entirely new level.

Even with training and clarity of roles, the interim time can be difficult for churches. Most churches see a decline in attendance and finances during the interim period. On rare occasions a church will actually grow during an interim period. Most potential members, however, would rather wait until a church has announced a new minister before they decide to join or become more involved. I have seen at least one instance where a church added new members almost every Sunday during the interim period and saw its finances grow. That is certainly, however, the exception.

> The interim time can be difficult for churches.

An interim time can be difficult, but with good, solid, trusted interim leadership, issues can be dealt with, grief and hurt can be healed, and the church can become increasingly ready for her new pastor.

But how does a church find an interim? This goes back to two chapters ago, and the same sources of information for pastoral candidates can also be possible sources of information for names of interims. Trusted friends and denominational sources can assist in providing names of trained and trusted interims. There may be a retired pastor who has previously served effectively as an interim pastor. A denominational person or local director of missions might serve. If there is a Christian college or seminary within the vicinity, that may also be a place to search for a good interim pastor.

On occasion, when a church is financially able, interims can be brought in from long distances. In my own experience, I have served as interim in four different situations and flew in on Saturday and out on Sunday, usually in all of these instances. I was available during the week by phone, e-mail, and Skype. The existing staff took care of local needs during the week. This can be done in some situations, but in most, because of financial and staffing issues, a local interim is sought.

The issue of job description for the interim must also be clarified. Does the church need an interim to handle day-to-day ministry responsibilities? If so, then the church must search for someone who is willing to relocate or someone who is already local. Do they need an interim pastor or an interim preacher? Do they need someone who is skilled to work with the committee and hopefully provide direction during the pastor search? That would be the optimal situation, and churches need to pray about having that kind of resource available whether the interim is local or long distance.

Question 5

How Do We Start?

 In the previous chapters, I have tried to share some important principles as well as warning signs. In question 2, "What Do We Need to Know?," I related a number of factors that should be on the front of your mind as the committee or team begins this process.

First Steps for the Committee or Team

Prayer

Most committees and teams begin with a serious season of prayer. I cannot overestimate the importance of this. The task that has been given to you is one of the most important that you will ever engage in throughout your entire life. It is an honor that you have been chosen for the task. Someone in the church feels strongly that you are a person who is spiritually mature and walking with the Lord for you to be in this place at this time. That is why it is vital for you to pray like you have never prayed before. William Vanderbloemen says it well, "Prayer moves the hands that move the world, and it's the single most important part of your search."[10]

> Pray like you have never prayed before.

In the winter 2015 issue of *Leadership Journal*, an article by Ben Tertin entitled "The Painful Lessons of Mars Hill" stated that "a pastor's character shapes the church."[11] In this article regarding the failure of a megachurch, the author is pointing out the desperate need for pastors and leaders "to stop obsessing over methodology and to cultivate the fruit of the Spirit in their lives." That is so true. Committees and teams must understand that a pastor's character does shape the church. Therefore, the committee members need to pray that God would lead them in this process of finding a new pastor who indeed will change the church's character and shape the future of the church.

To be honest, the actual process for the pastor search committee or team will differ from that of searching for a staff member of some other kind. But in every search, it is imperative that you *begin the process by prayer*; and then, when you have finished with that, spend more time in prayer!

I strongly believe in the reality of spiritual warfare. I have shared with my congregations repeatedly that we live in a battleground, not a playground. The spiritual warfare that is talked about in 2 Corinthians 1:3–5 and Ephesians 6:10–18 is a real part of our lives. I have found that spiritual warfare increases dramatically during the time of a pastor search. If there is any time when the evil one knows he can wreak havoc in a church, it is during this time. This is why prayer is vitally important.

I have also found that, in particular, the members of a search committee seem to be targeted by the evil one in many ways during this season. Members must pray one for another and over one another. Ask the church to pray for the committee members and the church like never before. This is said not to alarm but to warn you of the need to be deeper in prayer than ever in your entire life!

Personal Preparation

Every person on the committee needs to spend time seriously seeking the Lord for personal revival, renewal, and direction. Yes, it is an honor that you have been selected for this task. At times you may come to believe it is some kind of punishment; however, I hope you will always view it as a task from the Lord. If you feel woefully unprepared for the task, it is probably a good place to be, as it will cause you to lean on the Lord more than you ever have in your entire life. To recognize that the entire future of your church depends on your correct decision is a frightening reality, but it is also the truth. Spend time praying to the Lord. Make sure that sin is confessed and removed from your life. Maintain a walk with the Lord during this process deeper than anything you have done before. Ask the Lord to reveal to you areas of weakness that you need to work on. Ask those around you—family and friends to whom you are accountable—to help you in your own personal walk and make you aware of any area that needs improvement.

This could be one of the greatest seasons of spiritual growth in your life.

Above that, keep a journal for your personal walk. Keep a section of that journal to review how God walks with your committee and answers your prayers through the entire process. This is always a good practice and especially so in a season like this.

Identify the Needs of the Church

While this will be discussed more in chapter 6, it is extremely important to identify what the church really needs at this particular point in time. To start this process, the committee or team must have an awareness of where the church is during this particular point in her history. I strongly encourage a statistical study to see not only who your church is but also what your community is like. For example, what is the ethnic makeup in your church and community? Do they coincide? What age groups predominate your church body and community? What is the DNA of the church? Who is the church at its core? What style predominates the church's programs and worship? What are the needs of the community? Survey the community and ask what they are looking for in a church.

Boldly ask community leaders what they see the need being in that community for a church to make a difference. Not only do you seriously need to identify the DNA of the church, but you need to identify the DNA of the community.

> You need to identify the DNA of the community.

Many churches go about this process in a sloppy way and assume they know the reality of their own church when they do not. For example, some months ago I was in a strong church that was predominately made up of one ethnic group. I was hosted by a layman from the church who had been a part of the church for decades. I asked him about the ethnic makeup of the community as I had heard some interesting facts. He assured me that the community around the church was made up of his people group. When I talked to the pastor later on that day, he assured me that another ethnic group now made up almost 50 percent of the area surrounding the church facility. This is a prime example of a person who thought he knew the DNA of the community but was completely unaware of the changes that had taken place over the years.

Along with the statistical study, there is the issue of using a survey among your church members. Most pastor search committees or teams believe this is important. I believe it is also, but I encourage committees or teams to recognize that almost every survey taken reveals basically the same information. Almost all will agree to take the survey and will say they prefer a certain style of leadership and programming. Almost everyone states a certain age preference. If you look carefully, these surveys will reveal to you the true makeup or DNA of the church.

Surveys also provide a way for church members to feel they are part of the process. Yes, take the survey and ask what they wish for in their new pastor. Ask them questions about what they would prefer in education, age, family, skill set, and more; but please make sure you follow the leadership of the Holy Spirit, not the results of a survey. Remember also that the survey is taken among people of every spiritual maturity level. Don't be surprised what you find. Recognize that some members will take this as an importunity to be far more vocal than they normally might be, and your decisions might be led by a small minority of vocal people. The importance of recognizing this is so great. Please take a moment to reread this paragraph.

These conversations and surveys will provide a great avenue for you to discern who your church really is—an incredibly important task. Connected with that task is the issue of discerning the church's willingness to move forward and to even change in certain areas. What if the church's DNA is unhealthy in some way? Will they be willing to repent and move in a different direction?

> Follow the leadership of the Holy Spirit, not the results of a survey.

One very large church in the deep South went through a difficult time in the last few years when it was discovered they brought in a pastor to be a "change agent" and told that pastor the church was ready to make serious changes, but the reality was quite different. While the committee was willing to see changes made and even desired those changes to be made, the basic membership had no intention of seeing those changes occur at that time. Therefore, the pastor was brought in with an agenda and seeming permission to enact that agenda when the church body itself was resistant to that agenda. Thus, it is extremely important to recognize who your church really is and where they are in their willingness to see needed change occur.

Involve the Church

It is important that the committee not only involve themselves in personal prayer and diligently seek to identify the church's needs but also to involve the church in that prayer. Most search committees come before the church body at least monthly to give a progress report, but this report time should also involve a call to prayer.

Many pastor search committees share prayer requests with the church body that are specific to the stage in the search process. For example, the first month they can ask the church to pray for the discernment needed in identifying the church's true makeup, personality, and needs. This calls for the church to be deep in prayer. Later they can ask the church to specifically pray for the process of identifying the profile for the pastor. Accompanying Scripture verses should always be placed beside the prayer requests as the committee seeks this help from the body in order to assure church members that these prayer requests are sound and biblical.

In addition, it would be highly appropriate for the church to be in prayer as the committee begins to listen to Internet sermons and visit pastoral candidates. Involve the church in prayer at every step in the process. To have the entire church body aware of where the committee is and praying along every step of the way is an extremely important factor—not only in securing the results of prayer but also in helping the church stay involved all along the way.

As we have said before and will say again, an interim period is a time of spiritual warfare for any church. The evil one knows how to sow seeds of discourse during this time probably better than any other time in the church's life. If a church is engaged in earnest prayer, they will be far less likely to be involved in disunity, rebellion, and gossip. Ask the church to pray as they have never prayed before!

Logistical Matters

During the first few meetings, the search team or committee should concentrate on prayer, accumulation of information, and discernment of the church's present realities and needs.

Also, during the first few weeks, other tasks will be decided and developed. For example, decide which persons fill the officer positions on the committee. A search committee chairperson may already have been chosen, but if not, that should be done within the earliest meeting. In addition, a recording secretary should be elected within the committee. Keeping minutes of the meetings and making sure everything is organized is of extreme importance. Sometimes the chairman does this as well.

Decisions will be made about meeting times and dates. Almost every committee decides on a weekly meeting, especially at the beginning of the process.

Decide on basic ground rules. There should be a clear discussion and understanding of confidentiality. The committee must be careful to maintain strict confidentiality, not even sharing with their spouses the matters that are discussed within the committee. If the circle of knowledge is ever to be widened, it must be with the understanding of the entire committee.

There must be a decision made on the requirement, or lack thereof, for unanimous votes. Paul Powell in his pastor search committee handbook says that you should not require a unanimous vote. He says, "You can't know that everyone on your committee is walking with the Lord."[12] It is best to state publicly that you seek unanimity but do not require it, as you do not require it for any other vote in the church.

Question 6

What Do We Need to Look For?

In looking at this particular issue, I encourage each one of you to return to question 3, "What Should We Avoid?" Please reread this chapter and see the propensities of many search teams and committees. There are things you need to be aware of as you ask the question, "What do we look for in our new pastor?"

These tendencies and propensities have led many churches to make seriously wrong decisions. For example, they thought they had asked the right questions when, in reality, they had not even approached the most important areas. They trusted when they should have sought verification. They misunderstood their DNA and moved forward with a pastor who would help a church very different from the one they were a part of. It is vitally important that every search team or committee get these issues correct.

When a search team understands the direction they need to take, they can avoid the pitfall of thinking they will find a perfect pastor. Unfortunately, many people continue to think that such a creature exists! One humorous story notes the needed requirements for a "perfect pastor." (Author unknown. Sermon illustration, 1985.)

> He preaches exactly twenty minutes, then sits down. He condemns sin but never hurts anyone's feelings. He works from 8:00 a.m. to 10:00 p.m. in every type of work from preaching to custodial service. He makes $60 a week, wears good clothes, buys good books regularly, has a nice family, drives a good car, and gives $30 a week to the church. He also stands ready to contribute to every good work that comes along. He is twenty-six years old and has been preaching for thirty years. He is tall and short, thin and heavyset, handsome. He has a burning desire to work with teenagers and spends all his

time with older folks. He spends all his time with a straight face because he has a sense of humor that keeps him seriously dedicated to his work. He makes fifteen calls a day on church members, spends all his time evangelizing the unchurched, and is never out of the office.

Obviously, that is hyperbolic. It's a hugely exaggerated estimation of the expectations churches place on their pastors. But the reality is, many committees and church members have their sights set far too high.

How, then, do we set the bar high while remaining reasonable in our expectations? Remember, we are looking for a man, not Superman.

I have identified three key characteristics for which every church must look. The bottom line is that every church needs a pastor who is a leader, a preacher, and a caring pastor. Let's review these in more detail.

Characteristics of a Pastor

Leader

This aspect of a pastor's makeup cannot be overestimated. There are persons who can preach a great sermon and who may be great at pastoral care, but their leadership skills are extremely weak. Example after example of poor leadership has led many churches to flounder as staff and lay people are looking for someone to lead forth in vision, programming, and ministry. As I wrote in a book on leadership entitled *The Nehemiah Factor*, many people look to business writings to see the needed leadership qualities they wish for their pastor. This can be extremely helpful as there are transferable leadership qualities in both business and ministry. However, there is a spiritual leadership that is needed in the pastorate that is foreign to much of the business world. While much business leadership is helpful and useful, we must remember that much is also founded on a worldly wisdom that cannot transfer to the local church. We need leaders who have a heart for God. We need leaders who have the courage to step forth, even when a church, which is made up of volunteers, not employees, may seem somewhat timid about moving in a new direction.

Leaders know how to gauge the climate of a church. They know when to push and when not to push. They know when to commend and when to exhort. Leaders are constantly encouraging the people to move to a higher level of commitment and under-standing of the Bible. Godly leaders are constantly setting before the people a vision of where God would wish them to be.

I have written in several venues about the aspect of leadership known as charisma. Charisma is that innate, difficult-to-describe quality of leadership whereby a person is able to connect with a group of people at a level beyond logic or even description. This difficult-to-describe quality is sometimes called "presence." The French even have a phrase for it: "*je ne sais quoi.*" It is a quality which is hard to identify and rarely seen in its fullest sense, but it is very much present in the lives of great leaders.

> Leaders know how to gauge the climate of a church.

This charisma or presence gives a person an indescribable drawing power as it enables a pastor to bring along a body of believers to follow a vision that is more powerful than the person himself. That is truly the key definition of charisma: it gives a person the ability to lead because the task he is leading in or the vision he is proposing is more important than his own life. History shows many examples of charismatic men and women, some who have led in a positive way and some who have led in a horribly destructive way. However, their charisma cannot be denied. Winston Churchill, Nelson Mandela, and Mother Teresa were all incredible leaders who led in positive ways. But on the flip side, Adolf Hitler and David Koresh were arguably just as charismatic in their leadership, sadly causing ruinous and devastating outcomes.

Please mark my word: we need leaders as pastors. While it is true that leadership can be learned and leadership skills can be developed, you need someone who is willing to be a leader, who will take risks, and who also understands the basic tenets of leadership.

Preacher

The second of the three big needs for every pastor is his preaching ability. Obviously the ability to powerfully communicate scriptural truth and the biblical message cannot be overestimated. Some people used to joke and say that as long as a preacher cared about the people, he could get by with lots of poor preaching. While that may be true for some people, most in our twenty-first-century world want a preacher who can preach with effectiveness, power, and clarity.

Many issues are connected to this particular aspect of pastoral leadership. How long does a pastor preach? In our current milieu many young pastors like to preach for forty-five minutes or longer. While this is certainly nothing new, it is something the congregation needs to understand. If a pastor's normal style is to preach fifty minutes and your church requests a twenty-minute sermon (due to multiple services, television, or Internet schedule, or congregational preference), know that the pastor will likely end up reverting back to his normal style and length of preaching. Not only is the length of a pastor's sermon important to discern, but what style of sermon does he normally preach? For example, is he an expository preacher? Simply put, does he normally take one passage of Scripture and exegete the truths from that passage? Or does he preach topical sermons, preaching about one topic and using a plethora of scriptural texts to illustrate and expound on that topic? There are many styles of preaching out there. A team or committee must discern which style they find most comfortable and appropriate.

Does the pastor or candidate clearly and accurately expound on what Scripture is saying? Does this candidate connect Scripture with daily life? Are serious points of personal application brought forth from the pastor's preaching? Are you able to go away from the sermon with one key powerful thought? Are the sermons memorable? Are notes or multimedia presentations provided ahead of time to help a studious church member follow along? Does the pastor's presentation vary in vocal emphasis, or is it a monotonous presentation? Does he preach in such a way that every level of hearer is involved and challenged?

Questions about one's preaching style and ability cannot be overestimated in importance. Also remember what was said earlier in question 3: almost every preacher can come out with a good sermon every once in a while, but can this preacher, with consistency and regularity, preach sermons that are challenging to the congregation?

I hate that I must mention this, but you should check to see that the pastor's sermons are his own. While every preacher uses material from commentaries, other preachers, books, and articles, some fail to give attribution where necessary. Is the material actually his? Unfortunately even some high-level pastors have been found to use other pastors' sermons verbatim.

Caring Pastor

Every search team or committee needs to discern where the candidate is regarding his pastoral care skills; these skills enable one to truly care for those in the fellowship. Some candidates have strong leadership skills and powerful preaching ability but may not have the skills needed to pastorally care for a congregation. Unfortunately in some situations this is all church members care about and do not want to be led or even challenged from the pulpit. They want someone to "take care of them." If that is the situation in your church, then you are probably looking for someone who is a chaplain only. I say this not to disparage chaplains because they have a great place of ministry; however, the pastor of a church is not a chaplain. He needs to be someone who can lead and preach and at the same time pastorally care for the people.

In my ministry, I have found that people will follow a leader and listen to a preacher if they know the person is a pastor to them. I have often told the story of a vocal woman in a church I served many years ago who told me how unhappy she was because I had changed some things in "her church." She pointed out that she did not like the changes at all. With a sly grin she said to me, "While I don't like what you have done to my church, I know you love me, and I trust you— and by the way, it's working!" This dear saint of God was a person who never caused worry regarding what she believed or where she stood. She always let you know! However, she did know I loved her. The reality is that I had walked with her and her family through multiple experiences, some good and some bad. I had been a pastor who had stayed there for years. While she may not have agreed with all I had done as a leader or preacher, she understood that I truly cared about her as a human being.

People will follow a friend more than they will follow an office. In an age where authority is often not trusted, people must know that you care for them. Your position alone will not achieve their trust. It is extremely important that the person you are looking at has the ability and skills to pastorally care for a congregation. This does not mean that the pastor must be at every event. It does not mean that he must join family members during every surgery of every member. However, it means that the person knows how to provide pastoral care, whether it is through his own personal ministry or by developing a group of ministers who truly know how to expand the pastoral ministry of the church.

With that being said, there are some things every pastor must be willing to do. Is he willing to visit in the homes of the people as he has opportunity? Will he connect by telephone, e-mail, or in person when there is a serious need?

> People will follow a friend more than they will follow an office.

I used to call all church members on their birthday. Imagine the pastoral relationship this developed with the congregation. I also made it a practice to write personal notes to as many individuals as I could. For example, in every church, the week before Mother's Day, every person who had recently lost their mother received a handwritten letter from me sharing with them that I knew their first Mother's Day without their mother would be difficult and I was praying for them. Others received a similar letter the week before Father's Day. Every spouse received a letter during the week before the first anniversary of their spouse's death. In addition to that, even though I pastored churches that would be considered mega-churches, I visited hospitals at least once a week and made sure I was the pastoral visitor on times like Christmas morning. In fact, I would visit and be home before my girls even woke up and knew that I had been gone. It is important to have a pastor who connects with people. Investigate this characteristic carefully. Does this candidate truly connect with people? Is he willing to go out of his way to ensure that members feel cared for?

In one church I pastored, I discovered that the search committee had visited my previous church for weeks before I even heard from them. They stated that they watched me in hallway conversations and in interactions with children, young adults, and older people. They wanted to see how I related and interacted with individuals of every age. This was a church who truly wanted to know how the candidate connected with people. This is not a bad idea!

Where Do We Find Names?

When a pastor search committee begins its work, has thoroughly researched its church's identity and DNA, and has designed a process that will shield against many of the mistakes other churches have made, they are ready to begin asking, "Where will we get names for our search?" This is an excellent question and one that is rarely asked. One of the main reasons for this is that in most churches, a large number of résumés begin to flood

> A large number of résumés begin to flood into a church office.

into a church office the moment the knowledge of a pastor's resignation, retirement, or death is released.

As the committee discusses the process of finding candidates and reviewing hundreds of résumés, ponder this humorous, imaginative letter:

To: Jesus, Son of Joseph
        Woodcrafters Carpenter Shop
        Nazareth 25922

From: Jordan Management Consultants
        Jerusalem 20544

Dear Sir:

Thank you for submitting the résumés of the 12 men you have picked for management positions in your new organization. All of them have now taken our battery of tests; and we have not only run the results through our computer, but also arranged personal interviews for each of them with our psychologist and vocational aptitude consultant. The profiles of all tests are included, and you will want to study each of them carefully.

As a part of our service and for your guidance, we make some general comments. This is given as a result of staff consultation and comes without any additional fee.

It is the staff opinion that most of your nominees are lacking in background, education, and vocational aptitude for the type of enterprise you are undertaking. They do not have the team concept. We would recommend that you continue your search for persons of experience in managerial ability and proven capability. Simon Peter is emotionally unstable and given to fits of temper. Andrew has absolutely no leadership qualities. The sons of Zebedee, James and John, place personal interests above company loyalty. Thomas demonstrates a questioning attitude that would tend to undermine morale. We feel that it is our duty to tell you that Matthew has been blacklisted by the Greater Jerusalem Better Business Bureau. James, the son of Alphaeus, and Thaddaeus definitely have radical leanings, and they both registered high scores on the manic-depressive scale.

One of the candidates, however, shows great potential. He is a man of ability and resourcefulness, meets people well, has a keen business mind and has contacts in high places. He is highly motivated, ambitious and responsible. We recommend Judas Iscariot as your comptroller and right-hand man. All of the other profiles are self-explanatory.

We wish you every success in your new venture.

Sincerely Yours,
Jordan Management Consultants[13]

Past Protocol

In the past, an unwritten but well-understood protocol forbade ministers to apply for positions at churches. Why this was the case I do not know. What I do know, however, is that it was considered anathema for a minister to submit his own name or résumé to a church. While that may or may not be good, it led to the practice, sometimes less than honest, of seeking a friend to submit a résumé or nominate a person for service. While it may have seemed that this came as a response from a third party, often the pastor who was interested was the one initiating the résumé submission.

Along with this, it was also deeply frowned upon for a minister to ever talk about financial matters until the end of the process. It was considered most important that both the committee and the pastor discern God's call in the situation before mundane matters such as salary, vacation, or personnel policies were ever discussed.

Let me assure you, things have changed!

Present Practice

Things have changed in the past decades. It is often now seen as perfectly acceptable for ministers or pastors to submit their own names in the case of a pastoral vacancy. Again, whether or not that is seen as acceptable is something the committee needs to decide. As I have pondered this over the years, I believe direct submission is a more honest practice. However, if someone wants to recommend a candidate, I personally find that acceptable as well. Even many smaller churches will find themselves deluged with dozens of names and résumés.

If there is not a sufficient amount of names brought forth of the quality and level of expertise desired, most committees use other sources of information for those names.

For example, many churches will receive names from their own church members. Church members often have knowledge of a successful pastor or minister in some other location. While this can be helpful on rare occasions, usually those connections are family or friend oriented and may have baggage attached of which the search committee needs to be wary.

Every church can also depend on trusted friends, such as pastors of other churches or local directors of missions, who can assist in providing names. Contact those in the community who have been successful in their ministry and ask them to assist in providing names of those that have seen successful.

It is important to note that virtually every state convention as well as associational office maintains a list of persons who would like to relocate. Sometimes these state conventions will offer to meet with a church to discern their specific needs before unloading a file of résumés, most of which would never fit that particular church.

In addition to trusted friends, associations, and state conventions, most seminaries maintain a database of recent graduates and alumni who would like to relocate as well. Many seminaries have excellent resources for names or potential candidates.

There are other sources of potential assistance as well. As I have mentioned, it is extremely important for churches to rely on experts in the field of pastor search and to ask those experts to assist in providing a short list to the committee. When this is done, the expert, and in some cases, a company, can provide a vetted list of potential candidates, all of whom have the leadership, preaching, and pastoral skills the church needs.

Among the companies that are involved in these kinds of operations are Minister Search, Shepherd Staff, and Vanderbloemen Search Group. Please note that I am not necessarily recommending any of these companies, nor of these companies, nor am I guaranteeing their success in any search. I simply mention them as places where some churches, particularly larger churches, can seek assistance.

> It is extremely important for churches to rely on experts in the field.

Once enough names have been collected, then the committee begins to work to sort those names into categories, that might be described as "A," "B," or "C." Using the criteria which has been established in question 6, and certainly based on much earnest prayer, the committee begins to discern from the names those that might be considered most qualified and most acceptable. This process can get difficult, however, because of the vast number of candidates. The problem for many committees is having too many names.

Many search teams or committees will seek state convention or national entity assistance within their denomination to receive names of pastors of growing churches. These kinds of lists are available, but parameters must be given. What does one mean by a growing church? What size church are you intending to place on this list? In addition to this, many search committees will call a state convention executive director or local director of missions and ask for the names of pastors who are doing a good job, whose churches are growing, and whose churches have been seen as leaders in missions, evangelism, discipleship, etc. It is important to seek out those upon whom God's anointing rests.

In this scenario, churches seek to ignore all names sent to them or to ignore those who have sought a new place of ministry. These churches choose to go after a pastor who does not want to leave his current ministry. This has all kinds of considerations. There are churches who will ask a pastor to pray about a new location, but they simply do not want someone who is looking to leave. The reason for this may be obvious. If pastors want to leave their current church, why are they wishing to leave? While it could well be that they sense God's release from their current place of ministry and know that God is leading them to a new place, it may be that they are leaving to run from something or someone. It could also be that they are, as mentioned previously, using their current church as a stepping-stone to get to something bigger. How can you know that they will not view your church in the same way? Some churches are extremely wary of those who are seeking to leave and wonder why they are seeking to escape.

A church should carefully consider this kind of strategy. When a church goes after those who are happy in their present place of ministry, there is often a great deal of wasted time and energy. I know of one large church that was turned down by numerous pastors who were content and successful in their local places of ministry. At the same time, I also know of a church that used this particular strategy and experienced phenomenal growth after that pastor and committee felt God's leadership in the process.

Logistics for the Committee

If I might speak into the logistical area, it is vitally important that the committee send out an initial letter to those whose names have been submitted by an individual, an entity, a seminary, or a state convention. It is imperative that promises not be made to anyone but that a generic letter is sent stating that the church or committee has received the name and/or résumé. The letter should say that if there is further consideration, they will hear again from the committee. This letter should include a request that the candidate be much in prayer for the church and the committee and assure the candidate that the search team is much in prayer about God's will for the future of the church. Remember not to promise future contact unless the search committee is certain it will occur.

It is imperative that a pastoral job description be established. Even though we have discussed the three primary areas of pastoral responsibility, it is vital that a thorough job description be developed. Most candidates will not proceed further unless they have a job description that is clear. It should contain the following areas of consideration:

- Clarification must be given as to the style of preaching sought and the expectations of the congregation regarding preaching at certain services. Obligatory times of preaching must be clarified.
- Supervision of staff must be clarified. It must be in writing whom the pastor is to supervise and to whom he answers.
- Clarify expectations as to who leads the church in programming, ministry, vision casting, and overall direction.
- Share counseling expectations and issues.
- Discuss evangelistic leadership issues.
- Clearly communicate overall leadership expectations.

In addition to a job description, there must be a stated expectation regarding theological training, years of experience, etc. While these might not be part of an official job description, the committee must be clear in what they are looking for.

What Do We Ask?

When a committee has done its due diligence in regard to the issues discussed in the previous chapters and has found itself with a group of acceptable names, which might be considered a short list or list of top candidates, it's time to begin the interview process.

Many churches seek to work with only one person at a time. While this is commendable, other churches seek to interview several persons at a time until they discern which one might be the top candidate. Personally, I think this direction helps the committee see the quality of available candidates and clearly helps them discern more of what each candidate is really like. Additionally, it provides the committee or team confidence that they have truly found the best of the best.

One important note at this point: I have worked with committees and found them shocked when they begin to interview candidates, only to find out that the candidates are interviewing with multiple churches. I've even seen some committees shocked to find that those persons whom they were considering had left and gone to another church without telling them. It is extremely important to ask candidates if they are dealing with another church, and if so, at what level. If a committee is not willing to commit to only one candidate, the committee or team cannot expect that candidate to make a similar promise to them. It is helpful, however, even if both church and pastor are entertaining several options, to communicate that clearly up front.

When a committee has decided to interview, normally this is done first by telephone to begin the general conversation. Perhaps there have been e-mails back and forth to see if there is interest and to discern some general facts about the candidate or the situation. In our current environment, follow-up interviews are occasionally done by electronic means so the candidate can be viewed while the questions are being asked. This is extremely important, as it helps reveal many aspects about the candidate's personality.

Once there has been e-mail, telephone, and even electronic/visual communication, it is extremely important to have a face-to-face visit. Sometimes there are issues involved because of cost, travel, etc. However, it is crucial that the team sit down with the candidate somewhere that would be relatively private. It is at this time that the questions become more serious. See the appendix for a list of questions I suggest the committee ask. These are not set in stone and should be added to or removed according to the search committee or team's own desires.[14]

Certainly, the candidate's record and past performance will be studied. You need the same kind of information about his current church as you have gathered about your own. Look at all the issues and areas of importance.

Moving Ahead

Study His Performance and Record as a Pastor

Seek clarification regarding worship attendance, small group attendance, baptism numbers, and other additions. I cannot stress this enough. In a number of situations, I have seen contradictions between what a pastor says and what his church's annual profile says. In other words, some pastors exaggerate to the point of absurdity. Every committee must seek verification of all numbers given. The chief financial officer of my organization likes to tease and say, "In God we trust. In all others we audit and verify."

Review Where He Has Served and Terms of Service

Particularly, pay attention to gaps that might have occurred in the years or dates. Investigate to see where he might have been during those "silent" times.

Clarify His Educational Terms

Simply put, it is important that the committee or team understand what the initials mean when one is referring to educational degrees. In the world of pastors, one will find a bewildering amount of educational designations for varying degrees. Unfortunately, pastors are the world's worst at claiming degrees that may or may not be authentic or come from an accredited and reputable institution. It is vital that a team or committee vet the authenticity of degrees and understand what they actually mean.

For example, many pastors will have a bachelor's degree. Where is it from? What was the degree? Was it from an accredited institution? Why did they pursue that degree plan or career path?

Many pastors also have a master's degree. The M.Div. (masters of divinity) used to be the standard degree for pastoral ministry. It is an extensive degree and usually requires three or more years of post-college schooling. It is lengthy because it includes a large number of subjects. In recent years a plethora of other master's degrees have been developed that are more specialized but not as complete. For example, there are master of arts degrees in theology or biblical studies. Many of these are fine and are offered by seminaries and colleges. Be sure to check where the degree was received and, again, the reputation of the institution.

Doctoral degrees can be confusing. A number of doctor's degrees are sought after and attained. Perhaps the most common in today's world is the D.Min. or doctor of ministry degree. This degree is granted by many colleges and most seminaries. It is a specialized degree specific to pastoral, missions, or educational leadership. If it comes from an accredited and solid institution, it can assist the minister in increasing his skill level in particular areas.

There are also honorary degrees. These are often called a D.D. (doctor of divinity) or L.L.D. (doctor of letters). Some pastors have honorary doctor's degrees from various schools and insist on being called "Doctor." Normally a pastor who has an earned doctor's degree, particularly a Ph.D., never insists on being called "Doctor." Unfortunately, that is part of the ego of some of our ministers.

The highest academic degree is the Ph.D. (doctor of philosophy.) It is like the old Th.D. or doctor of theology. It is considered a research degree and is the highest granted at any academic institution, secular or Christian. Again, if a person has a Ph.D., the question should be asked regarding why he has such a degree. Does he feel a calling to teach? Has he taught at some point? The Ph.D. is indicative of much work and study and does display a high level of endurance and intelligence. This is sought after by a few churches; however, most churches believe the doctor of ministry is sufficient for their pastors.

Seek clarification as to what the degrees mean. Seek clarification that the degrees are verified. One large church in Florida was devastated when questions were asked about their pastor, and it was found that the degrees listed had never been granted.

Call References

It is important to use the questions in the appendix as the committee begins to deal with references. In addition, ask the references some of the following questions:

1. What is his work ethic? Does he pay his debts? Does he tithe?
2. Does he get along well with others?
3. What are his strengths and weaknesses?
4. How would you describe his preaching?
5. Tell us about his family.
6. Tell us about his staff relationships, deacons, church leaders, and laypeople.
7. Do you know of instances of his leading through a crisis or conflict within the congregation?
8. Do you know of anything we should know that we have not asked about specifically?

Contact not only the references the candidate gives, but contact other persons that would know the candidate. This involves some degree of risk. Most committees or teams seek to delay this until right before making a final decision, as it is possible for some of this information to get back to the candidate and to the candidate's present place of ministry. While being careful in this research process, it is imperative that a committee or team vet this candidate very carefully.

Contact other persons that would know the candidate.

One church that I worked with previously was shocked to find out that the candidate's own references said less than kind things about him. That was a rude awakening and quickly involved the elimination of that candidate from the process. Most of the time, references are handpicked persons who will certainly say only nice things about the candidate. That is to be expected. This is why it is incumbent on the team or committee to move beyond those listed and dig much deeper.

Coordinate a Second Interview

Once initial interviews have occurred, references have been checked, and educational attainments have been verified and understood, the committee or team is at a decision point. A second interview normally would not occur unless the committee has narrowed the search to one candidate. At this point, it is getting more serious. In fact, using terminology that most people understand, the "dating phase" is over! Now it is time to get engaged. This means deliberations have gone to a deeper level.

The second interview should be done in person by the entire committee with the candidate as well

> Now it is time to get engaged.

as the candidate's wife. This might be done in a local restaurant or a neutral location. You want to see how the pastor and his wife engage in their relationship. It is also good, at some point, to get to know the candidate's children, if he has any, and hopefully meet them in a home environment. Again, you want to see and learn the personality and interaction of that family.

Things are getting serious at this point, and it is imperative that the committee maintains its ability to be objective. Continue looking for clues that reveal the leadership abilities of the candidate. Ask the difficult questions, such as those included in the appendix of this book. Don't get lazy as you see the finish line drawing near.

This is also an important time to begin dealing with financial issues. It is essential to have a clear understanding of his current financial package. Expectations need to be clarified about vacations, continued education, conferences, etc.

Confirm in Writing

This is an appropriate time to write a kind letter to other potential candidates to inform them that God has led your committee to narrow the search to one person and that they are not that person. Affirm other potential candidates in their current ministry. Assure them of your continued prayers and love. However, make clear that you have moved in another direction. There are many pastors who have been deeply hurt after becoming engaged in a pastoral search discussion, then never hearing from the committee when a decision was made to pursue someone else.

In connection with this, on rare occasions churches seek to codify their decision with some kind of formal letter, and sometimes, yes, even a contract for employment. On rare occasions employment lawyers are brought in to assist this process. This is not recommended. However, once the committee has made a decision and an offer has been made for employment, or at least an offer is made for the candidate to come "in view of a call," the specific items about employment regarding salary, vacation, personnel policies, etc., should be codified in a formal letter from the committee to the candidate.

At this point, duties, job descriptions, etc., should also be clarified. Many pastors have gone to churches and later said the true and expected job description did not match the job description communicated in the hiring process. Make sure there is clarity and consistency.

How Do We Seal the Deal?

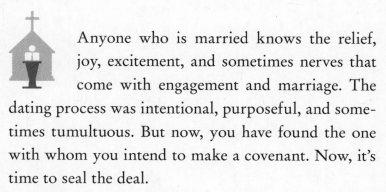 Anyone who is married knows the relief, joy, excitement, and sometimes nerves that come with engagement and marriage. The dating process was intentional, purposeful, and sometimes tumultuous. But now, you have found the one with whom you intend to make a covenant. Now, it's time to seal the deal.

The process of dating, getting engaged, and getting married can be a helpful metaphor for hiring a new pastor. Until this point, the committee has been "dating." At first, there were multiple candidates. The pastor was probably dealing with more than one option as well. As you would when pursuing a relationship, therefore, one of the first things to do when one gets serious with one pastoral candidate is to ask clearly if he is dealing with any other churches. It is vitally important that both the church and candidate are communicating with each other in a professional, honest, and Christlike manner.

Let me remind you of three key points of process:

- Prayer
- Discernment
- Decision

While your committee will continue to pray, and must, the first part of the search process was spent heavily on prayer and little on discussing other issues. As the process moved along, there came the time of receiving résumés and discerning the ones that were most suited to the church's needs. There was a serious time of determining what the church needed, sometimes using a survey, and always listening to church members and their opinions. The committee developed a church profile as well as the ideal candidate.

Then, the committee began phone calls, letters, sending questionnaires, listening and watching sermons online, and eventually going in person to hear various candidates. All the while the committee was attempting to discern which candidate might be the one, seeking God's will in the entire process.

At some point, it became evident to the committee, and hopefully all of the members, that one person stood above the rest. A decision is made to move forward with only one candidate. Certainly, when one is dating, one comes to the point of understanding he or she must commit to only one person, according to God's perfect will. As serious relationships develop, exclusivity is needed. This is true in the process of hiring a pastor as well. After one begins to make the decision to work with one person only, things become serious. As stated earlier, a series of interviews and visits can and should occur. Sometimes these occur over an electronic video or conference call. It is vitally important that a person-to-person visit happen so that both candidate and committee can discern the true fit for the situation. The initial visit is truly important and gives many clues.

However, the second visit or interview should become more serious. William Vanderbloemen stated it well: "It is vital that during this stage, just as in the interview process, you communicate openly with the candidate and not move too slowly."[15] He rightly points out that the candidate and the committee must be in regular communication. By this time, the candidate's heart and mind are beginning to move toward the new church. The people on the committee need to understand that a delay at this point in time can be hurtful and counterproductive to the minister and to the committee.

In this second or even third interview, things are now serious, and it is time for the committee to make a decision. Sometimes financial matters are discussed prior, but usually it is the second or third visit when the committee begins to focus seriously on the financial package. The chairman of the committee should have already secured from the candidate the information regarding what he is presently being paid in his current church. This gives the committee an idea of where they need to move regarding financial remuneration.

> A delay at this point in time can be hurtful.

With many search teams or committees, only a subsection of the committee deals with the finances. However, in many other situations, particularly in small churches, the entire committee is involved. At times, the church bylaws call for a personnel committee or deacons to become involved in the financial matters. Keep the group as small as possible. Even the pastor deserves a little privacy!

What should be included in this financial/salary discussion? Obviously, cash pay has to be established. Yet, ministers have different ways of dealing with salary. Most often a housing allowance is also provided. Still, to this day, the federal government allows a tax benefit for ministers, and a minister can use a portion of his salary as a housing allowance. This includes all expenses that are related to housing. Those are free from federal income tax.

> Even the pastor deserves a little privacy!

In many instances, particularly in rural areas, a parsonage is still used for the minister and family. This moment can serve as an opportunity for the church to consider whether or not to continue that practice.

While it may have been helpful at one time to give stability to a pastor who could not afford a home, churches need to understand that this could ultimately hurt a minister. While the house may continue to increase in value, does the church give the departing pastor that appreciated value? Usually they do not. In order to treat pastors fairly and generously, it would be wise for the church to give the incoming pastor an option on the parsonage and, if he accepts the offer, to give him and his family the appreciated value upon his departure.

Another issue that must be discussed is social security allowance. This is done because ministers have to pay the same amount as a self-employed person, which is extremely high. While they do receive a benefit from the housing allowance, it is almost taken away by the extra social security they are required to pay. Many churches provide a salary offset for social security reasons.

Insurance must also be discussed. Churches should include medical, disability, and life insurance. It is also vitally important that a church set aside retirement funds for their minister. It is recommended by GuideStone Financial Resources, the Southern Baptist retirement and insurance entity, that at least 10 percent is set aside for the minister and his family. The committee must also make decisions about reimbursement for travel expense, conferences, continuing education, books, etc.

As the committee continues to pray and discern through this "engagement" stage, there are many other things they should seek to discover. Following is a list of some of these things:

1. Goals and vision of your church that have been approved.
2. The ten-year record of your church that you have compiled.
3. Major problems in your church: aging or declining membership? Poor location? Internal conflict?
4. Profile of your community: growing suburb? Stable community? Declining inner city?
5. Evaluation of your present staff.
6. The potential for your church. Your growth expectations.
7. Condition of your church's facilities and needed additions and/or renovations.

8. Financial support, including expense reimbursements, protection coverage, and cash pay plus housing.

9. The candidate's administrative authority. Staff relations are a major source of conflict in churches. Who is in charge of the staff? What authority will he have over the staff? How will new staff be chosen and called/employed? Will he work with our present staff? If it is evident after twelve to eighteen months that one of the staff members needs to relocate, how will he handle the situation? How has he handled such a situation in the past?

10. Things that are sacred at your church—things that should not be tampered with, i.e., music program, pulpit furniture, schedule, etc.

11. Financial strength of the church, including debt and required payments.

12. Church's work expectations—office hours, days off, vacations, revivals.

13. How does the committee and church leaders expect him to relate to deacons and committees?

14. How does the church expect him to relate to the association and to the state and national conventions?

15. How does the church currently support missions, local and international, through various funding agencies?

16. What are the church's views of Sunday evening worship or any other schedule expectations?

17. The worship style the church is accustomed to and prefer.

18. How the vote for a new pastor will be handled.[16]

The candidate and committee should also recognize that references will be contacted at this time. As previously mentioned, it is important that the committee check with the persons listed by the candidate and also other persons who can give a clear portrayal of the candidate's character and performance.

Backgrounds checks must also be performed at this time. The committee will need to secure written permission from the candidate, but the following background checks are imperative:

- Financial and credit
- Education verification
- Criminal

As with salary, it is important to keep the number of committee members who see this information as small as possible. It must be decided up front what will be done with this information and who will hold it in confidence.

There is a great deal of excitement at this point in the process. Sadly, however, as many know from experience, it is at this point when the negotiations often break down. Decisions must be made, and, prayerfully, everyone on the committee would agree to move forward in a common direction. However, this is not always the case. Often, a disagreement on some terms of the offer will cause the process to be cut off, ending the engagement. If things do continue to go as planned, however, calendar dates can now be considered regarding when the pastoral candidate can come in view of a call.

When the committee and candidate reach this point, it is truly decision time. One hopes the pastoral candidate is ready to accept the invitation from the committee and the eventual vote and affirmation from the church body. As stated earlier in the book, church governance varies dramatically regarding the installation of the pastor, but there usually must be some kind of congregational affirmation when it comes to the calling of a senior pastor or minister. In almost every instance, when it reaches this point, it is virtually a done deal. Rarely do things fall apart on the actual weekend when the candidate preaches and meets the congregation for the first time. However, it is important to know that all the details must be cared for, and the committee must be firmly resolved that this is the right direction for the church to move forward.

Normally, when the weekend is established for the candidate to come in view of a call, a series of events is planned for the involvement of the candidate and his family with various groups in the church. Before we discuss the details of this weekend, it is important to note that in our age of rampant social media use, it is almost impossible to keep this kind of information from the church the candidate is currently serving. There is no way he could preach confidentially in view of a call without the other church and people knowing it. As soon as the name is announced, often a week or two ahead of time, someone in the other congregation will hear about it. This is why it is

> When it reaches some kind of congregational affirmation, it is virtually a done deal.

extremely important that a decision already be made in the hearts and minds of the committee and the candidate. This must be, in essence, a done deal because the other church will know he is considering leaving them, if not already made his mind up to leave. In view of that, many ministers now announce to their current congregation the week before that they are considering moving to a new church. This can be an awkward time, but it is very difficult in a day of instant communication to keep these kinds of things secret.

As the weekend is planned, normally the preparatory events include:

1. Individual meetings with ministerial staff during the day, followed by an evening social time with staff and spouses.
2. A meeting with the deacons and/or elders and their spouses.
3. Time of question and answer with church members or an open house when members can meet, greet, and question the pastoral candidate.
4. Breathing time allowed for the pastor and his family during the weekend. Be careful not to wear them out, even though it is a high-energy time that requires much interaction.

Another thing that can be done during the weekend is to have the age groups that correspond with the pastoral candidate's children reach out directly to his children with letters, calls, and specific events that might pertain to their particular age groups. This is an extremely helpful process that will help the candidate's family feel at home as quickly as possible.

The committee needs to be clear about what the church's bylaws or constitution say about hiring a pastor. If a simple majority report is called for, that must be presented clearly to the congregation. Also, the decision must be made whether to take the vote immediately following the morning service, to wait until the evening service (if the church holds one), or to hold a special church meeting. The morning crowd would obviously be much larger and give a far greater representation for the congregation's desires. Hopefully, there is deep respect for the pastor search committee's recommendation. If the vote occurs in the morning, normally, the pastor is brought back in to the congregation to accept the offer of employment to be the next pastor of the church. This is an exciting time and quite emotional in most settings.

Getting the Pastor to the Field

After the weekend of the pastor's official call, the work is definitely not over. There are many things that must occur to help the new pastor arrive and succeed in his early days. Usually, the search committee continues to work to assist the pastor and his family in their transition to the new location.

Some churches not only announce it to their fellowship but even use social media and other forms of media to announce their new pastor. The church will need to update their website and all church documents to share the good news of this decision.

Many churches hold a commissioning or installation service for the new pastor at some point after his arrival on the field. This can be a formal experience bringing in friends and supporters from previous ministries. It is also important for the committee to organize a beautiful welcome for the new pastor and his family. This can involve providing meals for the first few days/weeks, assistance with the move, and making sure they are aware of logistical details such as health professionals, auto services, grocery stores, restaurants, etc.

Many church teams and committees stay connected with the pastor as an ongoing, informal, if not formal, accountability and encouragement group. Perhaps they will meet for a meal at various intervals to assure the pastor of their continued prayers and support, and, if needed, for their observations and constructive criticisms. This is certainly a decision that will need to be made by the pastor search committee and the pastor. I would encourage it, as it helps the pastor continue to find his way in this new territory.

Once the pastor has moved in and begun the new job, the hard work has only begun! We will now turn our attention to what the church, particularly those leaders who were most responsible for finding and hiring the new pastor, must do to make the first several months as healthy as possible for the church and the pastor.

What Happens Next?

 So, you found the perfect one! He has been identified and voted in by your church and is now your new pastor. What happens next?

Celebrate with Thanksgiving

The first thing is to spend time praising the Lord for answered prayer. For months your entire congregation and search team have been praying. It is appropriate to spend time in celebration. When Nehemiah and his coworkers finished the work God had called them to, they celebrated the accomplishment! Nehemiah 12:27 says, "They sent for the Levites wherever they lived and brought them to Jerusalem to celebrate the joyous dedication with thanksgiving and singing accompanied by cymbals, harps, and lyres." While you may not use cymbals in your celebration, there needs to be a serious time of both personal and corporate celebration for the answered prayer!

Develop Support Network

Now is the time for you to come alongside your new pastor. In many cases the pastor search team or committee forms an informal, or sometimes formal, ongoing accountability, support, and encouraging network. During these first days, it will be important for the pastor to have a group of persons he can call on for advice, counsel, and prayer. Many people will vie for his attention, and many people with clear agendas will push for him to support those personal agendas and issues. It is vitally important for there be a group of church members who love him and his family unconditionally and stand by him during these days of adjustment and transition. Help him succeed in every way! This does not mean that you are to look blindly if mistakes or misjudgments are made. Remember to follow Matthew 18, and always approach him in private to encourage and help him in every way.

Understand Realities in the Twenty-First Century

It is also important for the search committee members to understand that doing church work in the twenty-first century is different than before. Many persons on the search team have been active church members for many decades and fail to understand how things have changed.

For example, I've often taught in church revitalization conferences that the definition of "active church member" has changed dramatically in the last decade or so. Not long ago, people thought they were active church members if they attended church twice a month or so. Probably, the only group who faithfully attends every Sunday these days is senior adults who are deeply committed to the church as an institution as well as a body of Christ. Every other adult generation sees church attendance as much less obligatory and less important than the senior adult "builder" generation does. The level of activity has increased dramatically in families and individual lives. Sporting activities, business trips, leisure activities, and academic opportunities have led many families to be far more active, particularly on the weekend. Even now in our culture, Sunday mornings have become prime time for athletic events. This would have been unthinkable decades ago in most parts of the country. Many, if not most, families now see themselves as active if they show up once every month or so.

What does this do for a church? Obviously it makes programming far more difficult. It also creates difficulty in maintaining growth. In fact, if a church is maintaining 5 percent level of growth for their history, doing that now requires adding double or triple the number of persons to join than previously required. Add to this the financial issue. Many people give to the church only when they attend. So, if a family is gone for multiple weeks in a row, the giving of the church can suffer.

Yes, this calls for serious programming emphasis and stewardship education. It calls for a pastor to be resolute in working with families and showing the importance of commitment in attendance and financial support. This can be done, but it has become more difficult than ever before. The pastor search committee or team needs to be strongly supportive of the pastor in the twenty-first century.

Closing Thoughts and Prayers

With all that being said, is there a guarantee that if you do everything recommended in this book that all will be great with the new pastor and his relationship with the congregation? Of course not! However, I trust you and each committee member will try. I hope you will take seriously the issues that have been discussed in this book. I pray that you will keep your eyes and ears open to Satan's constant inroads into the church. Pray daily for your pastor and your church that God will see His plan accomplished in your fellowship.

Having a new pastor gives a church a new opportunity. While we are all creatures of habit, this is a time for a church to perhaps break some old habits and develop new disciplines and correct patterns as the church moves forward. Encourage people to be accepting of the pastor's ideas and strategies. Pray that this would be a new day in the church—a new day that leads to far greater evangelistic fervor and purposeful commitment to discipleship and ministry. Calling a new pastor is truly a significant accomplishment and can be an occasion for new growth, new excitement, and new unity. Satan will fight this at every hand. Make sure God's people stay focused on God's plan, always keeping vigilant for the enemy.

As I write these concluding words, I am praying for you—that God will use you and your new pastor to see great things accomplished for the kingdom of God.

Appendix

Questions for Pastoral Candidates

Personal Issues

1. Please share your salvation story.

2. Please describe your call to ministry. Has this changed over the years?

3. Tell us about your family.

4. Describe your personality to us. How do others describe your personality?

5. Describe your wife's personality. How do others describe her personality?

6. Please tell us about your personal walk with God. Tell us of your prayer life and what you do regarding personal Bible study. What did you read today?

7. Share your personal evangelism habits and strategy. Tell us about the last person you won to Christ. When did this happen?

8. Tell us about your preferred study habits.

9. Tell us how you manage time. What are your priorities?

10. How would others describe your strengths and weaknesses?

11. What do you do for leisure or fun?

12. Talk to us about criticism. How do you handle criticism? Give an example of recent criticism and what happened to resolve the issue.

Scripture

1. Please describe your belief about Scripture.

- Do you believe it to be without error?
- What phrases or words would you use to describe Scripture? Specifically, do you believe it is relevant for the twenty-first century?
- Do you believe the Bible contains various types of literature, and would you consider any part of it to be mythical?

2. Please describe how Scripture has impacted your life.

Soteriology

1. Please describe your impressions of and feelings about reformed theology or Calvinism.

2. Please describe the five points of Calvinism and how you feel about each one of the points.

3. Please discuss how you feel this issue is impacting the convention and local churches. How has it impacted your life?

4. Please answer the following questions for those of us who are not as astute in this area as others:

- Do you believe God has foreordained the eternal destiny of persons regarding salvation and eternal life?
- Is it a predetermined, foregone conclusion where people will spend eternity?
- Do people have any role in accepting that destiny or not?
- Are there people in hell today that God did not wish to be there?

Eschatology

1. What is your view of the end times?

2. What role does your view of the end times have on your ministry and preaching?

Evangelism and Missions

1. Please describe the place evangelism and missions has in your life and ministry.

2. What evangelistic and missions influences have shaped your ministry?

3. Please give specific examples of how you have shared the gospel with individuals and how you pray for the lost.

Leadership

1. Please describe your leadership style.

2. Please tell us how others would describe your leadership style.

3. Please give specific examples of how you have exhibited leadership in your current place of ministry. What vision have you put forth, and how did you see that vision accomplished? How was it communicated?

4. Please discuss the issue of overall vision and how strategies are put into place to see that vision accomplished.

5. What are the greatest frustrations you've had in leadership?

Staff Relations

1. Please describe your philosophy of supervision. Do you find yourself supervising every aspect of a staff member's ministry, or do you seek to delegate? Please explain that process.

2. Discuss how you work with staff who exhibit a lack of competence or maturity. How do you help them, or how do you discipline them?

3. In worst case scenarios, where a staff member needs to move on, how do you help in this situation?

4. Please give specific examples of your overall staff relationship experience. Give specific examples of staff members with whom you have worked and how you have supervised them. How would they respond to the question, How is it to work with this pastor?

5. Please discuss staff enlistment. How would you go about hiring new staff? How would you get the names? Who would be involved in the process of hiring new staff? What standards do you use for ministerial staff and other staff?

Finances

1. Please share your overall philosophy regarding supervision of finances at the church.

2. Please share with the committee your feelings about disbursement of funds. Who should be in charge, who should approve, and how should finances be accounted for in the church?

3. Describe your personal financial philosophy. Have you been successful in your life in managing your finances? What will a credit report reveal to us?

4. Please share with the committee your view about tithing. Do you practice tithing? If yes, where do you tithe?

5. Please share your feeling about how a church should support missions and ministries, specifically your view regarding the Cooperative Program and also your view about how the church should do its own mission work. Share specific examples of how you have done this in the past and how you have led your church or churches.

Notes

1. *Religious Congregations Membership Study, 2010 Religious Census Report. Journal for the Scientific Study of Religion*, vol. 44, no. 3, September 2005, 307–22.

2. William Vanderbloemen, *Search: The Pastoral Search Committee Handbook* (Nashville: B&H Publishing Group, 2016), 17.

3. See Lisa Cannon Green, "Study: Lack of Support Reason Pastors Leave Pastorate," January 12, 2016, accessed February 16, 2017, www.bpnews.net/46126/study-lac-of-support-reason-pastors-leave-pastorate.

4. Billy Graham, *Just As I Am* (New York: HarperCollins, 2007), 399.

5. Ibid.

6. Vanderbloemen, *Search*, 55.

7. Not original. FSP used this illustration for years and pulled it from an old sermon illustration resource or another pastor. Found source on line with similar illustration: Michael E. Hodgin, *1002 Humorous Illustrations for Public Speaking* (Grand Rapids: Zondervan, 2004), 204, accessed February 16, 2017, http://bit.ly/2ik7WJD.

8. Bill Hybels, "Reading Your Gauges," *Christianity Today* (Spring 1991), accessed February 16, 2017, http://www .christianitytoday.com/pastors/1991/spring/91l2032.html.

9. See Russ Rankin, "SBC Pastors Polled on Calvinism and Its Effect," LifeWay.com, accessed February 16, 2017, http://lifeway.com/Article/research-sbc-pastors-polled-on -calvinism-affect-on-convention.

10. Vanderbloemen, *Search*, 5.

11. Ben Tertin, "The Painful Lessons of Mars Hill," *Leadership Journal* (Winter 2015), 18–22.

12. Paul W. Powell, "The Pastor Search Committee—a Guide to Finding God's Leader for Your Church," Union Baptist Association, accessed February 16, 2017, www.uba houston.org/filerequest/4616, p. 2.

13. "The Bell" newsletter, Snyder Memorial Baptist Church, January 25, 1985, Fayetteville, North Carolina.

14. See the appendix.

15. Vanderbloemen, *Search*, 109.

16. Powell, "The Pastor Search Committee" (adapted from).